Presented to:

_____

Presented by:

_____

Date:

_____

E-MAIL FROM GOD FOR TEENS

by

Claire Cloninger & Curt Cloninger

David C Cook

transforming lives together

E-MAIL FROM GOD FOR TEENS
Published by David C. Cook
4050 Lee Vance View
Colorado Springs, CO 80918 U.S.A.

David C. Cook Distribution Canada
55 Woodslee Avenue, Paris, Ontario, Canada N3L 3E5

David C. Cook U.K., Kingsway Communications
Eastbourne, East Sussex BN23 6NT, England

David C. Cook and the graphic circle C logo
are registered trademarks of Cook Communications Ministries.

LCCN: 00702739
ISBN 978-1-58919-810-4

© 1999 by Claire Cloninger & Curt Cloninger

Printed in the United States of America
First Edition 1999

8 9 10 11 12 13 14

021111

DEDICATION

For Kaylee and Caroline

Also for Jeanne, Claire, Anna, Jesse, Kitty, David, Edward,
Patrick, Pamela, Erin Claire, Daniel D., Chuck, Bonnie, and Leah

INTRODUCTION

Do you picture God as an old man with a white beard, drifting through the sky and dropping gloom and doom on the world? Do you see Him as a preacher in a three-piece suit, pounding a pulpit and yelling at the people in the pews? If so, I have good news for you! God isn't anything like those old stereotypes. He's real. He's alive. He knows your name. And He loves you!

Suppose you could sit in a chat room with God every day and ask Him anything. Suppose you could hear Him talking to you about your problems, your friendships, and all the decisions you have to make. You can! You can hear Him through His Word.

E-Mail from God for Teens speaks God's words in everyday language. It offers guidance, help, hope, good news, encouragement, and love. It's a chance for you to log on to God's heart and mind. So, what are you waiting for?

YOU WON'T MISS OUT

Lord, you have assigned me my portion and my cup; you have made my lot secure. The boundary lines have fallen for me in pleasant places; surely I have a delightful inheritance.

Psalm 16:5–6

Dear Child,

>Lots of people think that being a Christian means missing out on the good stuff. They think I'm the father who makes you ride your bike to school on your sixteenth birthday when everyone else gets a new car.

That's not Me. I have a wonderful inheritance for you. Read My will and learn that I've promised you the best slice of life. I've made you, so I know what makes you happy. I know you better than you know yourself.

So hang in there and trust Me. I've got something great for you, and it's not a rusty bicycle, I assure you. I'm the One Who knows how to bless you.

Your Maker,
>God

=== ================

YOU ARE GIFTED FOR A REASON

Be generous with the different things God gave you, passing them around so all get in on it.

| 1 Peter | 4:10 MSG |

– – – – – – – – – – – – – – – –

Dear Child,

>Ever think of the billions of people I've already made and wonder why I needed you? Is there a real purpose for your life? Trust Me, I gave every person special gifts—you included. Maybe you haven't found yours yet, but you will.

Some people are good managers. Some are good artists, or athletes, or teachers, or writers. I designed all people so their gifts would work to benefit others. The problem is, many people don't care two cents about anybody else. They use whatever talents they've got to make a better life for themselves. I hope you won't see things that way. Let Me help you discover your gifts and show you how to share them. You are gifted for a reason!

Your Creator,
>God

=== ===============

IF YOU REALLY LOOK, YOU'LL FIND ME

You will seek me and find me when you seek me with all your heart.

Jeremiah   29:13

— — — — — — — — — — — — — — —

Dear Child of Mine,

>Have you ever lost something that you didn't really expect to find again? Sure, you rummaged around the house looking for it, but since you didn't actually think you'd ever find it, you didn't really look with much hope or expectation. You know what happens in those situations? Since you don't expect to find it, you rarely do.

Some people look for Me like that. "Oh, God's out there, but He's so far above me, I'll never reach Him." Believe Me when I say that if you'll put your heart into looking for Me, you will find Me! I am so close to you. Open the eyes of your heart and really look. Expect Me to be here, because here I am.

Your Friend,
>God

=== ===============

I'LL NEVER GIVE UP ON YOU

For I am convinced that neither death nor life, neither angels nor demons, neither the present nor the future, nor any powers, neither height nor depth, nor anything else in all creation, will be able to separate us from the love of God that is in Christ Jesus our Lord.

Romans ▼ 8:38–39 ▼

—————————————

My Child,

>Have you ever thought that your good behavior could make Me love you more, or that your bad behavior could make Me love you less? You're not that powerful.

I already love you 100 percent! Your good behavior won't change that. And no matter how bad you are, I'll never stop loving you. Never! I sent My Son, Jesus, to endure an awful death so that you could be with Me. I chose you and bought you at a great price—the price of My own Son's life.

There's no mistake you can make that will cause Me to say, "That's it! I don't love you anymore!" You may give up on Me, but I'll never give up on you. I love you with a fierce love that knows no end.

Your Faithful Father,
>God

=== ===============

YOU ARE VERY GOOD

God saw all that he had made, and it was very good.

| Genesis ▼ | 1:31 ▼ |

— — — — — — — — — — — — — —

Dear Child of Mine,

>When I created this world, I looked around at everything I had made and said, "This is very good!" You are part of what I made, so you are a part of what I call "good." In fact, of all My creation, I'm most proud of you. Why? You were made in My image. You're like Me.

I put a lot of thought, creativity, and love into making you who you are. I have a plan and a purpose for your life. Even when you blow it, I still love you. You can make a mistake, but that doesn't make you a mistake. So whenever you fall down, just know that I can pick you up and start you over. You are "very good!"

Your Loving Creator,
>God

=== ================

LISTEN TO THE SONG I WROTE ABOUT YOU

The Lord your God is with you, he is mighty to save.
He will take great delight in you,
he will quiet you with his love,
he will rejoice over you with singing.

`Zephaniah`   `3:17`

—————————————

My Child,

>Have you ever thought about the fact that I like you? I don't just love you in some serious, religious way. I actually like you.

Have you ever seen a proud, first-time father with his toddler in the grocery store? That kid could be throwing all of the groceries out of the cart, and the dad's got this look on his face like, "That's my kid! Isn't he great!"

That's the way I feel about you. I'm showing you off to the angels up here. "Look! See My child! What a kid!" I sing songs to celebrate your life. You are My favorite, and don't let anybody tell you otherwise.

Your Biggest Fan,
>God

=== ===============

I WANT IT TO BE YOUR CHOICE

But if serving the Lord seems undesirable to you, then choose for yourselves this day whom you will serve ....
But as for me and my household, we will serve the Lord.

Joshua | 24:15

Dear Child,

>Did you ever wonder why I don't use My power to make people do what I want? I could have made the world like a big puppet stage and manipulated everyone by pulling on their strings.

But I wanted a real relationship with you. That's why I gave you a free will. I wanted you to have the freedom to choose Me. If I had to force you to love Me, would your love mean as much?

Sometimes you will make the wrong choices. But I'm willing to risk that, because when you finally choose My plans for you, I know it will be your decision. I'll know you have come to me because you really desire a relationship with Me and that you want this wonderful new life I have for you. That's the day I'll throw a party!

Your Loving Father,
>God

=== ================

I'M NOT THE OLD MAN UPSTAIRS

Surely the arm of the Lord is not too short to save, nor his ear too dull to hear.

Isaiah ▼ 59:1 ▼

Dear Child,

>When you think of Me, do you think of your grandfather? I'm pretty old, so lots of people think of Me as an old human being. I'm not. I sent My Son, Jesus, to show you My character.

Jesus was bold and strong—a carpenter from the age of twelve until thirty. After He entered His ministry, He defeated demons, He calmed a storm, and He turned over the tables of the money-changers in the Temple.

Think about Me as Jesus' Father; I created the whole world. I defeated entire armies with a wave of My hand. If you think I'm weak or deaf, you've got the wrong God, my friend. I hear you, and I am just waiting to help you. Call out to Me. I'm not your grandfather or your great-grandfather. I'm your Father, the Ruler of the universe. And I've got the power.

Your Heavenly Father,
>God

=== ===============

I TURN ON THE LIGHTS

God is light; in him there is no darkness at all.

🖼️ 🔗 🗑️ 📎 | 1 John ▼ | 1:5 ▼ | 🖊️ 📑 📊 🎞️

– – – – – – – – – – – – – – –

Dear Child,

>Have you ever walked into a bright kitchen and seen a patch of darkness floating in the middle of the room? Probably not. Light drives out darkness. It can't be dark and light in the same place at the same time.

Now think about light as goodness and darkness as evil. My Son, Jesus, is the brightest light ever. On earth, He walked through some of the darkest, most evil places in the world. And everywhere He went, Jesus turned on the lights. Once He met a man who was blind, literally surrounded by darkness, and Jesus restored his sight.

My Son wants to shine in your life, too. Just ask Him, and Jesus will drive out the darkness around you. Hey, that's what He does!

The Illuminator,
>God

=== ================

THERE ARE CLUES ALL AROUND YOU

**I'm single-minded in pursuit of you; don't let
me miss the road signs you've posted.**

Psalm 119:10 MSG

_____

My Child,

>I have posted obvious signs along your path that lead to Me.
Keep your eyes open—there is no way that you're going to miss
Me. I want you to find Me even more than you do. I've made the
way clear and straight for those who are really looking.

There are clues all around you—in the outrageously beautiful
world I made—in the diversity of people I created—in their
millions of different fingerprints and individual faces, voices,
and personalities. Best of all, I planted clues inside of your own
heart—a soft voice that tells you with every beat that I am real,
and I love you. Follow the clues.

Your Loving Father,
>God

=== ===============

YOU DON'T HAVE TO PROVE ANYTHING

Don't try to get into the good graces of important people, but enjoy the company of ordinary folks. And don't think you know it all!

	Romans ▼	12:16 TLB ▼			

_ _ _ _ _ _ _ _ _ _ _ _ _ _ _ _

My Child,

>You don't have to prove to other people how cool or popular you are, or elbow your way into the "in" crowd by pretending to be something you're not. Believe Me, you are a treasure to Me just because you're you.

It's your inner self that makes you valuable. I want you to learn to value yourself. You'll never be happy until you do. It doesn't matter how many "big shots" you impress, if you still hate yourself inside, you're going to be miserable. Find your worth in our relationship.

Learn to enjoy all kinds of ordinary people without putting on any kind of act. Each person is special and rare to Me—just as you are.

Your Creator,
>God

=== ===============

DON'T BE SCARED

**Let us draw near to God with a sincere
heart in full assurance of faith.**

Hebrews ▼   10:22 ▼

Dear Child of Mine,

>Have you ever stayed out past your curfew and then tried to
sneak in? If your parents caught you, you probably felt ashamed.

A lot of people approach Me in the same way. They feel
ashamed, so when they pray, it sounds something like this: "Oh,
God, I know you hate me. I'm so rotten. You'll never forgive me."
If you've done something wrong that you need to confess, tell
Me. Get it over with, and then come to Me with assurance.

Don't be scared. I'm your heavenly Father. Because of what
Jesus did on the cross, you can come to Me with confidence that
I'll always receive you. I'll always forgive you. I know what you've
done, and I love you anyway.

The One Who Accepts You,
>God

=== ===============

IT'S A JUNGLE OUT THERE!

A righteous man may have many troubles, but the Lord delivers him from them all.

Psalm 34:19

Dear Child;

>People are so confused about the way I work. They think My job is to get rid of all their troubles. I'm supposed to fix every bad situation and make every circumstance perfect.

Sorry. That's not My job. I will fix many of your circumstances, but you're still going to have some troubles. The good news is, as you get to know Me, you'll find that I am always with you. I will lead you through your troubles and out the other side.

Think of your life as a jungle, and I'm your Guide. I'm not going to turn the whole jungle into Disneyland. But I will lead you through the jungle. When your life gets wild, don't freak out. Just stick close. I'll get you through it.

Your Guide,
>God

=== ================

MY OPERATING INSTRUCTIONS

I tell you the truth, whoever hears my word and believes him who sent me has eternal life and will not be condemned; he has crossed over from death to life.

John   5:24

_ _ _ _ _ _ _ _ _ _ _ _ _ _

My Child,

>When you buy a new car, it comes with a little manual of operating instructions. That manual contains everything you need to know about taking care of your new automobile—what kind of gasoline is recommended, how often it will need servicing, and how much air pressure to put in your tires.

The words in the operator's manual are the link between the manufacturer and the car owner, and the extent to which the owner acts on those words will determine the performance of the car.

You get it, don't you? I made you. You are My creation. I am, in effect, the manufacturer of your life. But I have taken the risk of putting you into your own hands. My words for the care of My wonderful creation (you) are found in the Bible. Those words are life-giving. Read, believe, and take action.

Your Father,
>God

=== ===============

GOD DON'T MAKE NO JUNK

As for God, his way is perfect; the word of the Lord is flawless.

`Psalm` ▼ `18:30` ▼

_ _ _ _ _ _ _ _ _ _ _ _ _ _ _

Dear Child,

>You grow up expecting your parents to be perfect, and when you first realize that they're not, it's disappointing. After all, you trusted them. They taught you everything. They had all the answers.

But as the saying goes, "nobody's perfect"—except Me. I have never made a mistake, and I never will. Do you think giraffes were a mistake? Think again. I made them, and I'm perfect. Everything I do and say is perfect.

Do you think you're a mistake? No way! Remember, I don't make mistakes. I made you exactly the way you are for a reason. Stick with Me, and I'll show you why I'm so proud of you.

Your Creator,
>God

=== ===============

I KNOW WHAT WILL MAKE YOU HAPPY

It is obvious what kind of life develops out of trying to get your own way all the time: ... loveless, cheap sex; a stinking accumulation of mental and emotional garbage; frenzied and joyless grabs for happiness; trinket gods; ... uncontrolled and uncontrollable addictions.

Galatians | 5:19–21 MSG

_ _ _ _ _ _ _ _ _ _ _ _ _ _

My Child,

>The reason I don't want you to live a self-centered, self-seeking life is not because I'm a party pooper or an old meanie. It's because living like that will make you miserable. Guaranteed.

A lifetime of putting yourself at the center of your own universe will turn you into a caricature of low ideals and degrading habits. It will sink you into the mire of competition, trap you in a cycle of never-satisfied desires, and steal from you the joys of simple serenity.

I made you, and I know what will make you happy. You were designed to love other people and Me. That's where your happiness lies—not in an endless chase after selfish pleasures. Take My Word for it.

Your Heavenly Father,
>God

=== ================

I'M FUN

**Delight yourself in the Lord and he will
give you the desires of your heart.**

Psalm ▼ 37:4 ▼

— — — — — — — — — — — — — — —

Dear Child,

>Most people want a lot of "stuff" because they think it will make them happy. Think about it. You don't want a boat just to have a boat; you want a boat because of the fun you can have in it.

That's why some rich people who don't know Me keep buying more stuff. They think their possessions will make them happy, but it never works. If you spend time with Me, you'll find out that what you really want is a relationship with Me. I made you to need Me, and until you know Me, you won't really be happy.

Get to know Me, and I'll satisfy your desires. (I may even throw in a boat, too! You never can tell.)

The Joy-Giver,
>God

=== ===============

USE YOUR GIFTS CREATIVELY

Make a careful exploration of who you are and the work you have been given, and then sink yourself into that. Don't be impressed with yourself. Don't compare yourself with others. Each of you must take responsibility for doing the creative best you can with your own life.

Galatians ▼	6:4-5 MSG ▼

_____

My Child,

>I guess you've noticed that I didn't crank out a world of clones. Even if you looked in every city and town on the planet, you would never find another person exactly like you. You are an original, inside and out.

Part of your assignment as My child is to get to know yourself—what you're good at and what you like. This isn't a competition between you and anyone else. I don't grade on the curve. Be confident—you have a right to be. You're awesome!

Let Me help you discover how to use the gifts I've given you, performing work that you find exciting. I want to see your life count for something great!

Your Creator,
>God

=== ===============

I'M ALL FOR YOU

**What, then, shall we say in response to this?
If God is for us, who can be against us?**

Romans ▼ 8:31 ▼

My Child,

>Does it ever seem like your whole life is one great big contest? Or like every person you meet is grading you? Other kids are checking you out, sizing up your looks, your clothes, your personality, and your "cool factor." Teachers are grading your test papers with their red markers, ready to make a nasty slash across the slightest error. Parents are on to you about homework, curfews, and keeping your room clean.

Well, I want you to know that I'm for you, now and forever. So no matter what kind of "grade" you're getting with anyone else, you can walk around with this quiet, confident secret inside: "God is on my side."

Your Father and Friend,
>God

=== ===============

I KNOW YOU SO WELL

O Lord, you have searched me and you know me.
You know when I sit and when I rise; you
perceive my thoughts from afar.
You discern my going out and my lying down;
you are familiar with all my ways.

| | Psalm ▼ | 139:1-3 ▼ | | |

— — — — — — — — — — — — —

Dear Child of Mine,

>Sometimes you feel that no one understands you—that nobody
sees when you're happy and nobody cares when you're sad.
Your parents may seem too busy. Your teachers have their own
problems. Even your friends don't seem to be tuned into what
you're feeling.

But I know. I know you so well! I always have. I understand
everything about you—your joy and sorrow. All those thoughts
you want to express, but can't—I hear them, because I can listen
to your heart. I see, I hear, I care, I understand. Come. Talk to Me
today.

Your Loving Father,
>God

=== ===============

DON'T BE AFRAID

Say to those with fearful hearts, "Be strong, do not fear; your God will come, he will come with vengeance; with divine retribution he will come to save you."

Isaiah ▼ 35:4 ▼

— — — — — — — — — — — — —

My Child,

>Sometimes you've wondered where I am. You've said, "Doesn't God see what I'm going through? Where is He?"

I want you to know that I do care about you, and I am here to rescue you. This world can be a scary place, but I am in control. If someone is frightening you—a relative, a teacher, or a bully— pray to Me. Ask Me for help. I am the Father of the fatherless. That means if there's no one there to protect you, then it's My job to protect you. Hang in there! I'm on My way.

Your Protector,
>God

=== ===============

LISTEN TO THE WORLD AROUND YOU

The heavens declare the glory of God; the skies proclaim the work of his hands.

Psalm 19:1

My Child,

>Who do you think paints the sunsets? Do you think they just happen? Who do you think made the deep blue sky and the towering pine trees? Did they just "bang" into existence?

No picture paints itself. No building builds itself. So why would the world be any different? I made the earth and everything in it. Every blade of grass points to Me—the Creator. Every waterfall thunders My signature. Open your eyes and look around you. Creation didn't just happen by chance. I made it all.

And the greatest part of My creation is you. Take time to observe and enjoy the world I made, and before long, you will see My hand in all of it. I am the Author of it all.

The Creator,
>God

=== ===============

MIRACLES ARE STILL MY BUSINESS

You are the God who performs miracles; you display your power among the peoples.

Psalm ▼ 77:14 ▼

—————————————

My Child,

>Some people are looking for a big show of power from Me. Some think that if they could just see a miracle or two, they'd jump on the bandwagon and believe in Me. Well, plenty of people saw Jesus perform miracles when He was on earth. Some accepted Him, and some didn't. It's all a matter of what you choose to believe.

You are surrounded by miracles every day. Every time a flower blooms, it's a miracle. Every time a baby takes its first steps, or every time a husband and wife forgive one another, it's a miracle. I still do inexplicable and wonderful things every day—like multiplying food for the hungry and healing the sick. So keep your eyes open and choose to believe. Miracles are still My business!

The Miracle-Maker,
>God

=== ===============

I GIVE GOOD GIFTS

> Which of you, if his son asks for bread, will give him a stone? Or if he asks for a fish, will give him a snake? If you, then, though you are evil, know how to give good gifts to your children, how much more will your Father in heaven give good gifts to those who ask him!

Matthew ▼ 7:9-11 ▼

— — — — — — — — — — — — — — —

My Child,

>Parents aren't perfect, and some of them aren't exactly role models, but they at least have sense enough to feed their kids bread instead of rocks!

But I am the perfect Father. That means every time you want to talk, I want to listen. Every time you want to cry, I want to hold you. Every time you need advice, I want to give it. I know you can't see Me, but I am here. I celebrate your victories and grieve your losses. I write songs about you and sing them to you while you sleep. I brag on you to Jesus and the angels. I love you!

I give good gifts, so ask Me for what you need. I will never ignore or hurt you. I am so proud of you!

Your Loving Father,
>God

=== ================

DON'T MISS IT!

**Now this is eternal life: that they may know
you, the only true God, and Jesus Christ,
whom you have sent.**

John ▼ 17:3 ▼

— — — — — — — — — — — — —

Dear Child,

>You've probably heard a number of theories about how to
qualify for eternal life. Some people say only those who are
super good will make the grade. Other people are even more
legalistic about it. They say you have to work hard enough, be
good enough, belong to the right church, never miss a single
Sunday service, and watch your step day in and day out. They
believe that even then you can't really be sure whether you'll go
to Heaven.

Unfortunately, most of them are good people who just don't get
it. They're either killing themselves trying to be good enough, or
they gave up a long time ago, believing they'll never make it.

I wish they knew the truth. It's not that hard. Eternal life is based
on knowing Jesus and Me. I made it that simple because I didn't
want you to miss it.

Your Loving Father,
>God

=== ================

I CALL YOU BY NAME

"Woman," he said, "why are you crying? Who is it you are looking for?" Thinking he was the gardener, she said, "Sir, if you have carried him away, tell me where you have put him ...." Jesus said to her, "Mary." She turned toward him and cried out ... "Teacher!"

John ▼   20:15–16 ▼

—————————————

My Child,

>At school, have you ever been lined up by number instead of by name? Pretty impersonal, isn't it? Driver's license numbers, credit card numbers, and Social Security numbers are part of your everyday life.

It's so different when you hear your name spoken by someone you love! When Mary went to the tomb after the crucifixion, she found it empty and began to cry. But moments later, a familiar voice spoke one simple word, "Mary." Just hearing Him say her name, Mary knew Jesus was alive!

Listen for My voice. When I speak your name, you'll know that I'm alive in your life, too. You will never be a number to Me.

Love,
>God

=== ===============

CAN'T GET NO SATISFACTION?

> Jesus answered, "Everyone who drinks this
> water will be thirsty again, but whoever drinks
> the water I give him will never thirst."

John   4:13–14

Dear Child,

>In the Middle East during Jesus' lifetime, there was no running water. People had to draw their water from community wells.

One day, Jesus met a woman who had walked a long way from her house in town just to draw water from one of those wells. When Jesus told her that one drink of His special water would satisfy her thirst forever, it got her attention. To her, His promise meant she was free from her daily trip to the well. She didn't realize at first that Jesus was speaking of a spiritual principle. He promised her living water, and that's what I'm promising you.

I built you with a thirst for Me that only My Son, Jesus, can satisfy. The dirty well water of this world will never satisfy you. Turn on the faucet of Jesus in your heart. His love is like a cold drink—it satisfies!

Your Father,
>God

=== ===============

FRIENDSHIP IS A TWO-WAY STREET

I say: My purpose will stand, and I will do all that I please .... What I have said, that will I bring about; what I have planned, that will I do.

| Isaiah ▼ | 46:10–11 ▼ |

– – – – – – – – – – – – – –

Dear Child,

>Do you realize that I've existed forever, and I will always exist? I'm not just some illusion that you've dreamed up. I really do exist. Even when you turn on the television set or party with your friends, I'm still with you. You just can't hear Me then, because you're not paying any attention to Me.

I want you to get to know Me, but if you don't spend time with Me, how will you know My voice? Friendship is a two-way street. I love you and will always love you, but if you don't spend time with Me, how can you think of Me as a friend? I want to spend time with you. But it's your choice. I choose to love you whatever you do.

Your Father,
>God

=== ===============

YOUR SPIRIT WILL AGREE WITH MINE

God's Spirit touches our spirits and confirms who we really are. We know who he is, and we know who we are: Father and children.

Romans ▼   8:16 MSG ▼

————————————

Dear Child,

>I communicate through My Spirit. I know that's hard to understand. But My Spirit is communicating something majorly important to you right now. My Spirit is telling you Who I am. He's telling you who you are and Whose you are: I am your Father. You are My child.

It's so important for you to know and believe this. Check it out for yourself. If you turn down all the other noises in your life—the TV, CD player, and your computer video games—and get alone with Me, you'll know what My Spirit is saying: "Your Father loves you! Trust and believe."

Love,
>God

=== ================

THE BIBLE IS NOT A FAD

Heaven and earth will pass away, but my words will never pass away.

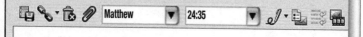

Matthew | 24:35

Dear Child of Mine,

>Your world is changing. To you, e-mail is new. To your great-grandparents, the telephone was new. To your great-great-great grandparents, "snail mail" was new.

As new things develop, old things pass away. All governments eventually fail. Even the earth and the sky will one day disappear. But My words in the Bible will never change. They always have and always will be true. They are just as relevant for you as they were for someone a thousand years ago. Circumstances may change, but truth is always truth.

If you are relying on a new fad, a new drug, a new president, or some new technology to make you happy, you're going to be disappointed. But if you rely on the Bible to guide your life, you will never go wrong. My Word doesn't change. You can count on it.

Your Everlasting Father,
>God

=== ===============

CLUB BEVERLY HILLS?

Dear friends, do not be surprised at the painful trial you are suffering, as though something strange were happening to you.

| 1 Peter ▼ | 4:12 ▼ |

My Child,

>Have you ever felt ripped-off or cheated about some little thing, and then felt ashamed because you saw starving kids on the news who had it a lot worse than you? It kind of puts things in perspective, doesn't it? Everyone has trouble, including Christians. So rather than complaining, ask Me, "What do you want me to get out of this experience?" Maybe you're suffering because of something you shouldn't have done. Ask, and I'll show you what it is.

But sometimes, if you are a follower of Jesus, you might suffer persecution just for who you are. Can you still trust that I'm in control? If you look at this world as a training camp, it's not such a bad place. But if you expect to spend your life at a country club, you're going to be one whiny camper. Everybody hurts sometimes. So hang in there.

Your Comforter,
>God

=== ================

FREE STEAK DINNER

**[The Lord] brought me out into a spacious place;
he rescued me because he delighted in me.**

Psalm ▼ 18:19 ▼

-- -- -- -- -- -- -- -- --

My Child,

>Whenever I hear people say, "Oh, I'm doing pretty well under the circumstances," I always want to say, "What are you doing under the circumstances? Get out from under there!"

I want your life to be better than just okay. I want it to be awesome! I know everybody has hard days sometimes. But My point is that it will always get better. If you're starving, a peanut butter and jelly sandwich tastes good, but a steak dinner tastes even better. I want to rescue you from your situation. It may take some time, but if you stick with Me, I'll lift you high above the circumstances. I want to bless you.

Your Father of Abundance,
>God

=== ===============

HOW ABOUT A FRESH START?

**Count yourself lucky, how happy you must be—you
get a fresh start, your slate's wiped clean.**

Psalm ▼ 32:1 MSG ▼

My Child,

>A lot of kids act like there's no right and wrong. They've got a
"do whatever feels good" attitude. But when those same kids go
against their consciences, I guarantee you, they feel guilty. They
may not let you know about it, but they do. They try to stuff the
guilt down deep inside and end up getting mad at Me. It nags at
them, so some of them take pills or start drinking to drown out
My voice.

The only real way to lose the guilt is by asking Me for forgiveness.
I'm the only One Who can let you off the hook. The good news is,
I can and will erase your wrong every time. You can start fresh,
just as if it never happened. So if you feel guilty about some of
the things you've done, bring them to Me. I'll always forgive you.

Your Best Friend,
>God

=== ===============

MAKE KNOWING ME YOUR GOAL

What is more, I consider everything a loss compared to the surpassing greatness of knowing Christ Jesus my Lord.

Philippians ▼ 3:8 ▼

My Child,

>It's one thing to know about someone, but it's a different thing to really know that person. For instance, you know about the President of the United States, but if you dropped by the White House today, you probably wouldn't get invited to lunch.

My Child, Job, knew about Me. But after he had an encounter with Me, it was a whole different deal. The Apostle Paul's one goal in life was getting to know Jesus. In fact, he considered everything else a big pile of trash compared with that goal.

Maybe, like Job, you've heard about Me all your life. Maybe you can sing "Jesus Loves Me" with the best of them. But that doesn't mean you know Jesus or Me. To know Us is to enter into a relationship with Us. Make that your goal.

Your Friend,
>God

=== ===============

I WANT TO AMAZE YOU

Call to me and I will answer you and tell you great and unsearchable things you do not know.

Jeremiah | 33:3

— — — — — — — — — — — — — — —

Dear Child of Mine,

>Part of the fun of being God is blowing people's minds. I'm serious! I know everything, and every now and then, I'll share something deep with one of My children. I love watching their eyes pop open as the light goes off in their heads and they say, "Wow, I get it!"

I have some of those eye-opening revelations that I want to share with you. I've created you to understand and appreciate things about Me that no one else will ever know. I want to share it with you and only you. Spend time with Me and call on Me. Read My Book. Then listen and prepare to be amazed.

Your Maker,
>God

=== ===============

THE GIFT OF CONTENTMENT

Keep your lives free from the love of money and be content with what you have, because God has said, "Never will I leave you; never will I forsake you."

| | | | Hebrews ▼ | 13:5 ▼ | | |

Dear Child,

>Have you heard the battle cry of the world—"more, More, MORE?" Have you seen the "troops" lining up outside the mall, manned with their credit cards, ready to attack! Doors open ... ready ... charge!

That army is always looking for recruits, but "more" will not buy you happiness, whether it's more money or more stuff. But I have a gift that will bring you happiness. It is the gift of contentment. To be content is to feel glad about where you are with what you have. Rich? Okay. Poor? Okay. Plain? Okay. Fancy? Okay. To be content is to take your eyes off of money and stuff and turn them on Me. Let Me shower you with the riches of My love.

Your Source,
>God

=== ===============

YOU WERE MADE TO LOVE ME

**The Spirit of God whets our appetite by giving
us a taste of what's ahead. He puts
a little of heaven in our hearts
so that we'll never settle for less.**

2 Corinthians | 5:5 MSG

— — — — — — — — — — — — —

Dear Child,

>Sometimes you feel a deep sadness inside that you may
not be able to understand or explain. Everyone feels that way
sometimes. It's a longing for Me. You were created for fellowship
with Me, and nothing will fully satisfy that emptiness inside but
My friendship.

You'll have many other friends in your lifetime. That's good. I
want you to enjoy them. But you need to know that there is a
God-shaped hole in your heart that nothing but My love for you
will fill. And here's something that may surprise you: there is a
you-shaped hole in My heart that nothing but your love for Me
will fill. No matter how many other people love or follow Me, I'll
never stop waiting for your love. You were made for Me.

Your Friend,
>God

=== ===============

WILL YOU LOVE MY WORLD WITH ME?

Dear friends, since God so loved us, we also ought to love one another.

| 1 John | 4:11 |

Dear Child,

>In the beginning, My world was a little jewel of a planet with fields and forests full of amazing animals, waters full of fascinating fish, and skies full of glorious birds. But My masterpiece was the human family.

My plan for human beings was that they live forever in harmony with each other and Me. But they wanted their own way instead of Mine, so now there's a lot of sickness and sadness in My once-beautiful world.

Why don't I just wave a magic wand and fix it? Magic wands are not My thing. I work through people like you, who will love the lonely with My love and reach out to the broken with My touch. I need your heart to care, your hands to heal, your feet to go, and your voice to tell the truth. Will you love My world with Me?

Your Creator,
>God

=== ================

MY PATH IS NARROW, BUT NOT THAT NARROW

**You broaden the path beneath me, so
that my ankles do not turn.**

| Psalm | | 18:36 | |

My Child,

>Grace is a word you need to understand. Grace is Me giving
you more than you deserve. It's Me cutting you some slack.

Some people feel that obeying Me is like walking across Niagara
Falls on a tightrope. One mistake—one wrong move—and down
they go. But they've got it all wrong. I've built you a highway
across Niagara Falls. Sure you'll make mistakes, but you'll never
fall out of My grace. How will you ever learn to walk straight if I
shoot you down for every single mistake you make? Trust Me.
I'm not like that.

If you do the wrong thing, just ask for My forgiveness, get up,
and try again. I am for you, not against you.

The Forgiver,
>God

=== ===============

MY SON'S LOVE IS A LIFEBOAT

**I tell you the truth,
he who believes has everlasting life.**

John	6:47

_ _ _ _ _ _ _ _ _ _ _ _ _ _

My Child,

>Long ago, a huge British ship called the Titanic was hit by an iceberg on its maiden voyage. The Titanic was considered man's unsinkable masterpiece, and yet it sank. Hundreds of lives were lost, drowned in the icy sea, because the ship was not prepared for the emergency. There were not enough life jackets or lifeboats for everyone aboard.

Everyone will face death sometime, but I have a life jacket for you. It is My truth. I have a lifeboat for you—it is the mercy and love of Jesus Christ. I will not make you put on the life jacket. I will not make you climb into the boat. But I have prepared them for you.

If you will wear the life jacket of My truth and climb into the lifeboat of My Son's mercy, you will live. Come on. Get into the boat!

Your Lifesaver,
>God

=== ===============

DON'T JUST HEAR, TAKE ACTION!

Do not merely listen to the word, and so deceive yourselves. Do what it says.

James ▼ 1:22 ▼

My Child,

>By now you should know I'm a take-action kind of God. And nothing would make Me happier than getting you in on the action. Here's how it works. When you feel Me nudging you to do something, don't fool around. Do it! When you sense Me giving you directions, follow them!

This is where the adventure begins. Listening for My voice and then doing what I say is exciting. It's a secret just between you and Me. But be sure of this: I will never contradict myself. I'll never tell you to do anything that goes against what the Bible says. I'll never tell you to do anything Jesus wouldn't have done. That's why it's important for you to read the Bible and know My Son.

Ready to try it? This is going to be fun!

Your Friend,
>God

=== ===============

IT'S OKAY TO START SMALL

Now he began teaching them again about the Kingdom of God. "What is the Kingdom like?" he asked. "... It is like a tiny mustard seed planted in a garden; soon it grows into a tall bush, and the birds live among its branches."

Luke ▼ | 13:18–19 TLB ▼

– – – – – – – – – – – – – –

My Child,

>My kingdom is amazing and wonderful. It beats any magic show you've ever seen! It begins in a person's life as a small seed of faith—about the size of a sesame seed on a hamburger bun. It looks so insignificant that nobody pays any attention to it at all. Nobody but Me, that is.

My eyes are constantly on that seed of faith. I watch as it's planted in the rich soil of My love and mercy. I am constantly coaxing and urging and encouraging it to grow. Little by little and bit by bit, your faith begins to bush out, develop branches, and take on leaves. Then one day, people look in amazement at you—a "beautiful tree," creating shade, safety, and beauty in My world. Plant your faith in My love today.

Your Seed Sower,
>God

=== ===============

HAVE I GOT A PLAN FOR YOU!

"For I know the plans I have for you," declares the Lord, "plans to prosper you and not to harm you, plans to give you hope and a future."

Jeremiah   29:11

–––––––––––––––

My Child,

>Sometimes it seems like everyone, including your friends, your parents, and maybe even yourself, has a plan for you. Well, I have a plan for you, too. I created you with it in mind. It is your destiny—the reason you exist.

We have adventures to go on, you and I. There are new friends for you to meet and new places for you to explore. There will be tough times, but I'll give you strength; and when you're lost, I'll show you the way back home.

So when you need to make a decision, pray first and then listen. You will hear My voice like a whisper inside yourself. Trust Me. I only want to bless you.

Your Trail Guide,
>God

=== ================

CHURCH IS COOL

I love the house where you live, O Lord, the place where your glory dwells.

Psalm ▼ 26:8 ▼

_ _ _ _ _ _ _ _ _ _ _ _ _ _ _

Dear Child,

>I live with My children. Does that mean I live in a building? Well, when those who love Me and follow My Son, Jesus, are meeting in a building, I'm there, too. There's nothing I like better than to show up and be in the middle of things! But when they leave, I follow them home. Why would I want to hang around an empty building?

Wherever My people are, even when they're alone, that's where you'll find Me. But if you really want to see Me in action, go to one of their meetings where they praise and worship Me. Find a church full of happy, loving people who are excited about Me. It's a blast! See you there!

Your Faithful Father,
>God

=== ===============

BIGGER THAN THE BOOGEY MAN!

**The Lord is with me; I will not be afraid.
What can man do to me?**

Psalm | 118:6

Dear Child,

>Have you ever been spooked while walking alone at night? Maybe there was a noise in the bushes or a dog was barking, and it just scared you.

Now what if you had been out walking with a friend? You probably wouldn't even have noticed the barking dog. Things just aren't as scary with a friend by your side, so let Me walk with you.

I am everywhere all the time, and that means I am with you always. I am your best Friend. You are never alone.

So think about Me the next time that you're afraid. Let My nearness dissolve your fear. You don't need to be frightened anymore.

Your Best Friend,
>God

=== ==============

CHANGE STATIONS TODAY

I can do everything through him who gives me strength.

Philippians ▼ 4:13 ▼

Dear Child,

>Don't listen to that old radio station in your head that keeps singing yesterday's hit: "I can't, I can't, I can't." Change stations today! Tune into Me and get the sound of the truth going inside you.

The truth will sing a totally different song. The words go like this:

There's nothing you can't do! Anything and everything is possible. When you trust Me, I'll give you strength to see—there's absolutely nothing you can't do!

Once you get hold of that powerful reality, you'll see locked doors fly open. You'll find solutions to problems that used to look hopeless. And you'll realize that it's Me working in you, strengthening you, and helping you do what needs doing. Tune into My truth today!

Your DJ,
>God

=== ===============

MY KIND OF PERSON

**But Jesus called the children to him and said,
"Let the little children come to me, and
do not hinder them, for the kingdom
of God belongs to such as these."**

Luke 18:16

Dear Child,

>Have you ever wondered who I like to hang out with most? You might think it would be kings or presidents—powerful people who call all the shots. Wrong! You might think it would be the most religious people—the ones who could make 100 on a Bible quiz. Wrong again. Maybe you'd guess sports stars or movie stars.

No, not really. I'm not impressed with money or fame.

The people I love to spend time with are the ones with childlike hearts—the ones who are not always pushing into the spotlight, but who want to let somebody else shine. I have a heart for the ones who are willing to take a back seat and not act like know-it-alls—the ones who wait for My words and listen for My voice. Are you My kind of person?

Your Loving Father,
>God

=== ===============

I'LL BE THE JUDGE OF THAT!

You, therefore, have no excuse, you who pass judgment on someone else, for at whatever point you judge the other, you are condemning yourself, because you who pass judgment do the same things.

Romands ▼ | 2:1 ▼

Dear Child,

>Every time you start criticizing someone else, that criticism boomerangs and comes around to hit you in the head. Every time you act as judge and jury for someone else, you end up putting a noose around your own neck. Every time you point your index finger at someone else, look at your hand. There are three other fingers pointing back at you.

Listen, there's only one Person on the judging committee, and that's Me. I'm the only One Who can look inside a heart and see its motives. I'm the only One Who can pour out grace undiluted by prejudice. When you judge someone else, you just end up judging yourself. So give other people the benefit of the doubt and leave the judging to Me.

Your Father of Grace,
>God

=== ==============

PRESCRIPTION FOR A GOOD LIFE

**Whoever wants to embrace life and see the day
fill up with good, Here's what you do:
Say nothing evil or hurtful; Snub evil and cultivate
good; run after peace for all you're worth.**

---

1 Peter ▼   3:10–11 MSG ▼

Dear Child,

>Want a prescription for a good life? I've got one, but don't
expect anything supernatural. It's plain old common sense. Here
it is: Don't run off at the mouth with harmful gossip and mindless
chatter. You can hurt other people with your words.

When you see your friends headed for trouble, turn around and
run in the other direction. It's not worth being part of the crowd if
the crowd is getting ready to throw itself off a cliff. It doesn't take
a rocket scientist to figure out that reckless, dangerous choices
lead to a reckless, dangerous life.

So run away from what's bad for you, and run after what's good.
You'll be rewarding yourself with peace and happiness, and your
regrets will be few. Trust Me!

The Author of Common Sense,
>God

=== ===============

I WILL BE CHEERING YOU ON

When you give to the needy, do not let your left hand know what your right hand is doing, so that your giving may be in secret. Then your Father, who sees what is done in secret, will reward you.

Matthew ▼	6:3-4 ▼

_____

My Child,

>Jesus loved to see His followers doing good things for others, but He warned them not to be show-offs about it. His warning is still in effect.

It's not necessary to act super holy to impress other people. Be quiet about the good things you do. It's more fun that way. Even if no one else sees your good deeds, I'll notice. My eyes of love will be on you. Your good deeds will be our secret—yours and Mine.

I'm watching and cheering you on and giving you the quiet reward of My approval. I'm pulling for you!

Your Rewarder,
>God

=== ===============

JESUS MADE YOU INNOCENT

Therefore, there is now no condemnation for those who are in Christ Jesus, because through Christ Jesus the law of the Spirit of life set me free from the law of sin and death.

Romans | 8:1–2

My Child,

>I want to talk to you about some deep stuff. Because My Son, Jesus, died for all your wrong thoughts, words, and actions, you're not guilty anymore. But the devil still wants you to feel guilty, so he condemns you. In other words, he makes you feel bad about yourself for no specific reason.

Sometimes when you do something wrong, I'll cause you to feel bad about that one thing so you'll tell Me you're sorry. But I'll never make you feel bad about who you are. That's different. I love who you are, and if you've asked My Son to live in your heart, you'll feel My love.

I want you to be free from feeling bad about yourself and free from doing bad things. That's why Jesus died for you—to set you free! My love will always lift you up!

The Lord of Freedom,
>God

=== ================

WISDOM IS AS WISDOM DOES

For wisdom is more precious than rubies, and nothing you desire can compare with her.

| Proverbs ▼ | 8:11 ▼ |

———————————

Dear Child,

>You know, there are people with genius IQ's that still can't make a friend or get a date? To be smart and to be wise are two different things. Wisdom is knowing Me and living like I'm in control. It's one of the most valuable and desirable traits to acquire.

In the movie, *Forrest Gump*, Forrest is kind of slow; but his mom loves and believes in him. She tells him, "Stupid is as stupid does." I agree. I'll go on to say, "Wisdom is as wisdom does." You don't have to make straight A's to be wise.

So how can a young person gain wisdom? Read My Bible, particularly the book of Proverbs. It will make you wiser than some of your teachers. Don't wait until you're old and gray to be wise. Seek wisdom now.

The Source of All Wisdom,
>God

=== ================

WHAT DO YOU WANT ME TO DO FOR YOU?

"What do you want me to do for you?" Jesus asked
him. The blind man said, "Rabbi, I want to see."
"Go," said Jesus, "your faith has healed you."
Immediately he received his sight and
followed Jesus along the road.

Mark ▼ 10:51–52 ▼

_ _ _ _ _ _ _ _ _ _ _ _ _ _ _ _

Dear Child,

>My Son has good manners. He would never push His way into
your life, changing and rearranging everything, without your
permission. He waits to be invited in, and then He waits to hear
what you want.

"What do you want Me to do for you?" He asked a blind man,
and the blind man answered, "Rabbi, I want to see." This man
had enough faith to ask for what he wanted, so Jesus didn't fool
around. He answered the blind man's request immediately, and
the blind man regained his sight. And more than that, he began
to follow Jesus.

What do you want Jesus to do for you? Do you want to see Him?
Believe in Him? That's one request He wants to answer. All you
have to do is ask.

Your Father,
>God

=== ================

WHO WILL I BE TO YOU?

**"But what about you?" [Jesus] asked.
"Who do you say I am?" Simon Peter answered,
"You are the Christ, the Son of the living God."**

Matthew ▼ 16:15–16 ▼

My Dear Child,

>I'm not a gray-haired old geezer, sitting on a rusty throne in
Heaven. I'm alive! I'm a powerful, present-tense Person, who
loves you with a powerful, present-tense love. I was, and I am,
and I will be forever. I am the unchanging Word of truth.

I can tell you Who I am. But only you can say Who I will be to
you. I want to be your Father (a good Father Who's involved
in your everyday life), your Friend (a Friend Who knows your
strengths and weaknesses and is always on your side), your
Savior (the One Who comes to your rescue in everyday
problems), and your Guide through the tricky maze of life. It's
your call. Who do you say that I am?

The Great I Am,
>God

=== ================

YOU CAN BE REAL WITH ME

There is a friend who sticks closer than a brother.

Probverbs ▼ 18:24 ▼

--- --- --- --- ---

Dear Child of Mine,

>Everybody needs one friend they can be real with—no faking it, no putting on, no trying to act like who you are not, and no hiding who you are. I want to be that Friend to you.

I know who you are, and I like you anyway. I like the way you think and talk and smile. I like your sense of humor. I want to spend time with you—just the two of us. You don't have to learn some super-spiritual way of praying. Just talk to Me! I want to hear what you have to say. You don't have to act super holy or perfect. Just be totally honest with Me. I want to be with you, not some character you've invented to impress Me.

I'm the One Who invented the real you—exactly as you are—and I like My work!

Your Friend,
>God

=== ===============

DIVE INTO PRAYER

**God's Spirit is right alongside helping us along.
If we don't know how or what to pray,
it doesn't matter. He does our praying in and for
us, making prayer out of our wordless sighs.**

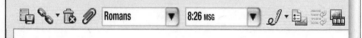

Romans	8:26 MSG

— — — — — — — — — — — — — — —

My Child,

>Prayer is an ongoing adventure. Dive into it like you would a deep, clear river and swim! Don't worry about knowing how to pray. My Spirit will be there to keep you afloat. He is the ultimate prayer partner. He prays with you, in you, and for you.

Sometimes you'll have a nagging feeling that there's something you need to pray about, but you can't seem to put your finger on what it is. That's when My Spirit goes into action. He sees what's in your heart—all those things you can't put into words—then He turns your sighs into prayers. And even though you may not know exactly what He's praying through you, I will know. And I will answer.

Your Prayer Partner,
>God

=== ================

I WANT YOU TO MEET MY FRIENDS

**If one falls down, his friend can help him up.
But pity the man who falls and has no one to help him up!**

Ecclesiastes ▼ 4:10 ▼

My Child,

>Just a word of advice: make good friends. I've designed
humans to need each other. No one is strong enough to succeed
on his own. Even professional athletes have managers and
agents. Needing friends doesn't make you weak; it just makes
you human.

You can tell good friends by how they treat you when you fall
down in life. Do your present friends ditch you in bad times?
Then you need new friends.

A church is a place where My family comes together to love Me
and to love each other. A person who truly loves Me will stick
with you when you run into tough times. In fact, I have some
incredible new friends I want you to meet. And they need you just
as much as you need them!

Your Friend,
>God

=== ===============

IT'S MY WORLD

**Every animal of the forest is mine, and the cattle
on a thousand hills. I know every bird in the mountains,
and the creatures of the field are mine ...
the world is mine, and all that is in it.**

| Psalm | 50:10-12 |

My Child,

>The earth is mine, and I created everything in it. I personally
made every single atom in the universe! And I own everything,
even the things you think you own.

The reason I ask you to give your time and money to Me is that
it proves to both of us that you love Me more than you love what
I can give you. I know what your priorities are by how you spend
your time and money. Do you know what comes first in your life?

The good news for you is that I love you, and I will take care of
you. You don't need to worry about going broke. Your Father
owns everything!

The Creator,
>God

=== ===============

THE BEST FOOD IS FREE

**Come, all you who are thirsty, come to the waters;
and you who have no money, come, buy and eat!
Come, buy wine and milk without money and without
cost. Why spend money on what is not bread,
and your labor on what does not satisfy?**

Isaiah | 55:1–2

––––––––––––––

Dear Child,

>A lot of people think that becoming a child of God requires
following a bunch of impossible religious rules. "Yeah," they
grumble, "I would live for God, but He doesn't want me. I can't
be good enough anyway." What a lie!

Most free stuff is crummy. But My free gift of Heaven, where you
will live in joy for eternity, is the most valuable present you'll ever
receive. All you have to do to get to Heaven is to believe in and
follow My Son, Jesus. And to have My power in your life, you just
need to let Jesus sit in the driver's seat and take control of your
life. That's it! Simple, isn't it?

Stop buying the moldy bread of this world, and come feast on
My love for you. It's free!

Your Host,
>God

=== ===============

IT GETS BETTER, I PROMISE

Weeping may remain for a night, but rejoicing comes in the morning.

Psalm ▼ 30:5 ▼

-- -- -- -- -- -- -- --

Dear Child,

>Unfortunately, sadness is sometimes a part of life on earth. I didn't create the world that way, but when men turned against Me, the world took a turn for the worse.

So there will be some times in your life when you are just plain sad. Jesus' friends were sad when He died; but then He came back to life, and they had a party. I work that way a lot. Sometimes things get worse before they really get better.

So when you're sad, just hang in there. In time, your sadness will lift. Even Jesus was sad. But He laughed and smiled a lot more than He cried. There may be some sad parts to the movie of life, but it has a happy ending. I promise.

The Creator of New Life,
>God

=== ===============

LET'S GET TO KNOW EACH OTHER BETTER

In your presence is fullness of joy; At your right hand are pleasures forevermore.

| | Psalm ▼ | 16:11 NKJV ▼ | |

Dear Child,

>Have you ever had a crush on somebody? You know how it is; every time that person walks into the room, you get excited. If that person sits near you or talks to you, there's nowhere else that you would rather be. If that person goes to a party, you want to be there.

That's what I want our relationship to be like. I'm a person. I have a personality. As you begin to know Me better, you'll see. There's nothing in the world like being in My presence. As you set aside time to be alone with Me, expect it to be exciting. There are personal things I want to tell you. There are plans I want to share with you. I want to know you better. And I want you to know the joy of knowing Me. So let's spend time together!

Your Best Friend,
>God

=== ===============

LIVE CAREFREE!

Live carefree before God; he is most careful with you.

| 1 Peter | 5:7 MSG |

My Child,

>Is your life filled with worry? Do you find yourself getting stressed out over everything from tomorrow's English assignment to the price of chewing gum? That's no way for anyone to live, much less one of My children. I want you to wake up every morning feeling carefree, knowing the happiness that comes naturally to the child of a loving parent.

Have you ever noticed how babies in the arms of their mothers will sometimes throw themselves backwards, certain they will be caught? Or how toddlers jump from a high place into the waiting arms of their fathers, never doubting they'll be caught? That's the kind of carefree trust I want you to have in Me. Don't worry. Be happy!

Your Joy-Filled Father,
>God

=== ===============

DON'T GIVE UP

So let's not allow ourselves to get fatigued doing good. At the right time we will harvest a good crop if we don't give up.

| Galatians ▼ | 6:9 MSG ▼ |

My Child,

>Sometimes the temptation to quit is overwhelming. When you feel beat and burned out, it seems like nobody cares whether you keep trying or not. Well, there's something I want you to hear loud and clear. I care! Never forget that for a minute.

In the midst of all your challenges, I'm with you. Life is a big tug-of-war between the call to care about others and to do good, and the temptation to quit. Quitting says that nothing matters and life is a throwaway. When you hang in there and "keep on keeping on," you affirm My call on your life to make a difference.

So, dig in, and stand up. I've got you covered, and I won't let you go. Don't give up! I love you.

Your Encourager,
>God

=== ===============

SAY "YES" TO LIFE

**But he took [the dead girl] by the hand and said,
"My Child, get up!" Her spirit returned,
and at once she stood up. Then Jesus
told them to give her something to eat.**

 Luke 8:54–55

— — — — — — — — — — — —

Dear Child,

>Sometimes the hardest thing in the world is not facing some big, heroic challenge. Sometimes the hardest thing is just getting up, getting dressed, and saying "yes" to life.

Eating breakfast, brushing your teeth, and putting one foot in front of the other is difficult when you want to pull the covers back over your head. It's easy to get discouraged and start feeling down on yourself or down on life.

On days like that, I want you to remember how much I believe in you. On days like that, I want you to hear My Son, Jesus, saying to you, "Get up! It's a new day, and I'll be with you in the midst of everything." If His love was powerful enough to raise a dead girl to life, don't you think it's powerful enough to give you the hope and energy you need for today? Say "yes" to life.

Your Life-Giver,
>God

=== ===============

YOU CAN'T, BUT I CAN

**With your help I can advance against a troop;
with my God I can scale a wall.**

Psalm | 18:29

My Child,

>If you will do the possible, I will do the impossible. In My book, the Bible, a soldier named Jonathan tracked a huge army of enemy soldiers and defeated them all with only the help of his butler. Two guys beat a whole army!

Was Jonathan a Superman or Rambo? No, he was a fairly decent soldier, but he was just a person. Jonathan did what he knew was right. He fought the enemy. I did the rest.

If you will step out and do what you know needs to be done, I will finish the work you start in My name. Are people hungry in your town? Begin feeding a few of them, and I will help you feed the rest. I will tell you to do things that you can't do. But don't be afraid. If you start it, I'll finish it.

Your General,
>God

=== ================

WHO ELSE IS LIKE ME?

There is no one like you, O Lord, and there is no God but you.

| 1 Chronicles ▼ | 17:20 ▼ |

_ _ _ _ _ _ _ _ _ _ _ _ _ _ _ _

Dear Child,

>I guarantee that you've never met anyone else like Me. I'm not bragging; it's just the truth.

Haven't I always forgiven you when you asked? Does anyone else know every thought you think and every dream you dream? Do you know anyone else who wants to be with you twenty-four hours a day? Has anyone else ever created a whole, beautiful world for you to live in, or created the air you breathe? Does anyone else have an exciting purpose for your life? Do you know anyone else who has prepared a home for you in Heaven, where you will never fear or hurt again?

I am the only One Who loves you in this way, and I want to share your life with you.

The One and Only,
>God

=== ===============

THIS IS NOT A SECRET CLUB

I have called you friends, for everything
that I learned from my Father
I have made known to you.

John   15:15

Dear Child,

>When people talk behind your back, don't you hate it? It's like they're saying, "Oh, it's an inside joke; YOU wouldn't get it." There's nothing worse than being left out of a group when you want to fit in.

Here's good news: Jesus won't ever keep secrets from you. He came to earth so He could tell you every single thing about Me. He came to tell you about Heaven. He came to share My love with you.

Christianity is not some secret, exclusive club. All you have to do is want to join, and you're in. I've chosen you to belong. I sent My Son to invite you. Come and hang out with Us!

Your Friend,
>God

=== ===============

RUN AWAY! RUN AWAY!

The name of the Lord is a strong tower; the righteous run to it and are safe.

| Proverbs ▼ | 18:10 ▼ |

My Child,

>Where do the good guys run to in the movies when the enemy storms the castle? The knights pull up the drawbridge, retreat into the inner tower, and wait it out. When your enemy is on your case, sometimes the best thing to do is run.

The devil is a pretty smart guy, and if you try to defeat him in your own strength, you'll probably fail. He knows your weak points. He knows how to tempt you. When you feel like you're under attack and things are getting crazy in your life, run to Me. I will fight the battle for you.

Sometimes the best offense is a good defense. When you're feeling weak, run into the tower. As you pray to Me and read My Word, I will guard you from the enemy. Run to Me!

Your Strong Tower,
>God

=== ===============

INVEST IN STRONG FRIENDSHIPS

**As iron sharpens iron,
so one man sharpens another.**

| Proverbs ▼ | 27:17 ▼ |

Dear Child,

>Some friends dull the edge of who you are just by hanging around you. They are time-wasters and procrastinators. Their thoughts are negative, their goals are shallow, and their ideas are weak.

Other friends sharpen you and bring your life into focus. They know what matters and what life is all about. They're not afraid to take a stand on spiritual issues—issues that count. You become a better person just by being around them. Their strength sharpens your character, and as you become stronger, your strengths sharpen theirs.

Invest your time, energy, and friendship in this second kind of friend. You won't regret it.

Your Best Friend,
>God

=== ================

BE CREATIVE

Sing to the Lord a new song; sing to the Lord, all the earth.

Psalm | 96:1

My Child,

>Have you ever seen the exact same sunset twice? It has never happened, and it never will. I've got a million of them. I never run out of new creations. I made you in My image, and I want you to be creative like Me.

Say new prayers. Sing new songs. It's great to have prayers and songs that other people have written. They help when you're stuck or you can't think of anything new to pray or sing. But every now and then, get off by yourself and sing Me a new song. It doesn't matter how it sounds. Just sing what's on your heart. It will sound great to Me, and you'll feel better, too. Be creative. I am.

Your Creator,
>God

=== ===============

IT AIN'T OVER 'TIL IT'S OVER

Those who sow in tears will reap with songs of joy.

Psalm | 126:5

My Child,

>Do you know the story of "The Little Red Hen"? She kept
breaking her back to bake this cake. None of her friends would
help, but she didn't let that stop her. Finally, the cake was
finished, and all her friends wanted a bite. But she said, "No way!
I worked on this cake; now it's my time to enjoy it."

My son, Noah, was the same way. I warned him of a coming
flood and told him to build a huge boat. So he got busy. Only one
problem—up until that time, it had never rained once on earth.
Also, Noah was landlocked. There was no water in sight. His
friends thought he was an idiot; but when the flood came, they all
drowned.

So, if I tell you to do something, just hang in there and do it.
Believe Me, you'll be glad you did!

Your Coworker,
>God

=== ================

START OFF ON THE RIGHT FOOT

Satisfy us in the morning with your unfailing love, that we may sing for joy and be glad all our days.

Psalm ▼ 90:14 ▼

—————————————

Dear Child of Mine,

>Some people are morning people. They wake up early and energetic, have a mega-breakfast, and get going. Some people are night people. They don't really get moving until noontime, and they do their best thinking late at night.

Which one am I? I'm both, because I never sleep. I'm thinking at night, and I'm up early in the morning. Whether you're a morning or a night person, here's My suggestion for you—right when you get out of bed, take some time to commit your day to Me. If you start your day off with Me, it will surely go better. When you remember that I have everything under control, you'll be much more likely to ask for My help during the day. Try it.

The Inventor of Time,
>God

=== ===============

THIS BOOK'S FOR YOU!

For the word of God is living and active. Sharper than any double-edged sword, it penetrates even to dividing soul and spirit, joints and marrow; it judges the thoughts and attitudes of the heart.

Hebrews ▼ 4:12 ▼

My Child,

>The Bible is not an ordinary book. It's My Word, and My Word is alive with power! Through its pages, I can teach you, help you, comfort you, and make you strong. My Word is a drink of cold water when you're thirsty or a safe place when you're afraid. It's a warm fireside when you're cold or a road map when you're lost.

You can know what is in other books, but My Word is a book that knows what is in you! So read it when you need wisdom or hope. Open its pages every day, and you'll begin to see that My Word is for you, right where you are ... today.

Your Father and Friend,
>God

=== ===============

YOU ARE SALT AND LIGHT

**You are the salt of the earth ....
You are the light of the world.**

| Matthew | 5:13-14 |

Dear Child,

>Have you ever tasted food with no seasoning at all? It's blah and tasteless. That's what people taste when they bite into a daily diet of life without My love. My love adds the flavor that makes life spicy and delicious. When you follow Me, you are salt for a bland and flavorless world.

Have you ever walked into a dark room and groped around trying to find the light switch? That's how lots of people feel every day in a world without My light. When you believe in Me, you become a flashlight, shining My light into the darkness so people won't stumble and fall.

You bring light by shining My truth into the hype, half-truths, and outright lies that flourish in this world. Will you be My salt and light?

The Light of the World,
>God

=== ================

A SHEPHERD WITH A PLAN

You were lost sheep with no idea who you were or where you were going. Now you're named and kept for good by the Shepherd of your souls.

1 Peter   2:25 MSG

————————————

Dear Child,

>Picture a rough, dangerous, uncharted road heading up into craggy hills where wild animals live. Now picture yourself as defenseless as a lamb—no weapon, no map, and no guide—unsure of where you are or where you're going.

Not a comforting picture! But that's a fairly accurate portrait of you before Jesus entered your life. What a different picture He wants to paint of your life if you'll let Him! He knows you, He loves you, and He has a new life for you. He has a road map through those dangerous mountains. He wants to lead you to a place of peace, joy, and happiness with Me.

Jesus is your Shepherd, and He's waiting to lead you. Won't you trust and follow Him?

Your Father,
>God

=== ================

I'M WAITING TO BE FOUND

Ask and it will be given to you; seek and you will find; knock and the door will be opened to you. For everyone who asks receives; he who seeks finds; and to him who knocks, the door will be opened.

`Matthew` ▼ `7:7–8` ▼

‒ ‒ ‒ ‒ ‒ ‒ ‒ ‒ ‒ ‒ ‒ ‒ ‒ ‒ ‒

My Child,

>I've heard you talking about Me with your friends: Is there a God? Isn't there a God?

Aren't you getting a little tired of all the talk? Aren't you ready for some truth?

I've got answers for you, if you think you can handle them—not merely intellectual answers, but real, honest-to-God, experience-it-for-yourself answers. Remember when you were a little kid and you used to play hide-and-seek? Maybe you found a great place to hide, but deep inside you were really longing to be found.

Well, I'm like that. I want to be found. So stop all the mental gymnastics, and put your faith in gear. Ask Me. I'll answer. Knock. I'll open the door. Look for Me. I'm waiting to be found.

I Am,
>God

=== ================

I WANT TO FORGIVE YOU

**For if you forgive men when they sin against you,
your heavenly Father will also forgive you.
But if you do not forgive men their sins, your
Father will not forgive your sins.**

Matthew	6:14–15

--- --- --- ---

My Child,

>I want to forgive you, but sometimes I can't because you won't forgive someone else.

If a group of kids cusses at you, and you hold a grudge about it, it's just the same as if you walk around all day cussing back at them. But as soon as you forgive and release them, you are released to receive My forgiveness. Don't worry about paying them back. That's My job. But I don't want to pay them back; I want to forgive them just like I want to forgive you! If you want Me to have mercy on you, have mercy on other people. If you want Me to give you a break when you blow it, forgive other people when they blow it.

When you forgive someone else, watch My love flood into your life. I've got a dump truck full of love and forgiveness that I want to pour out on you. Forgive—it's the best thing to do.

Your Dad in Heaven,
>God

=== ===============

THE CALL TO CARE

So we're not giving up .... Even though on the
outside it often looks like things are falling
apart on us, on the inside, where God
is making new life, not a day goes
by without his unfolding grace.

2 Corinthians	4:16 MSG

My Child,

>I know that sometimes it's tempting to give up on life.
Sometimes it's hard to fInd a reason to keep trying.

What makes you feel like throwing in the towel? School? Grades?
Friends? Parents? Money? War? Listen, I want you to trust Me on
this one. Even though the circumstances of life might look rotten
from the outside, when you believe in Me, there are invisible
things going on inside of you. Every day, I'm unfolding something
new and exciting. Your future will be more amazing than anything
you can imagine. Believe Me, it will be worth hanging on for.

So hang tough. Don't give up! I've got some real surprises for
you.

Your Heavenly Dad,
>God

=== ===============

THROW OUT THE CATALOG

What kind of deal is it to get everything you want but lose yourself? What could you ever trade your soul for.

Matthew ▼   16:26 MSG ▼

————————————————

Dear Child of Mine,

>Suppose life was like a mail-order catalog, and you could just flip through the pages, selecting everything your heart desired: computers, cars, clothes, fancy vacations, fame, money, power—no limits.

Only the day your order was delivered, it came with a bill that said, "Payment required: Your eternal soul." Would you still place the order? Lots of people do. But they don't fully understand the trade they're making. To begin with, the catalog is a rip-off. It will never deliver in full anyway. And even if it did, no amount of stuff would ever satisfy your soul's restless longing for Me.

So throw out the world's catalog and open up the pages of My plan for you—the Bible. My love delivers what it promises!

Your Loving Dad,
>God

=== ================

I BUILT THE CAR

The Lord will fulfill his purpose for me; your love, O Lord, endures forever— do not abandon the works of your hands.

Psalm ▼ 138:8 ▼

————————————

My Child,

>I have a personal interest in your success. You are My creation—a one-of-a-kind original. I've invested creativity, hope, and energy into making you who you are, and I have no intention of quitting on you now.

You're like a finely tuned race car that I've built. On the day of the race, don't you think I'm going to drive that car to victory? I'm not just going to leave it stalled on the side of the road somewhere. I belong in the driver's seat of your life, so put Me there by believing and trusting Me. I know the loops and curves of the track.

I have a plan for your life, child, and I am deeply committed to the results of your race. Don't worry. I haven't abandoned you, and I never will.

Your Driver,
>God

=== ================

CHOOSE LIFE!

**This day ... I have set before you life and
death, blessings and curses.
Now choose life, so that you ... may live.**

Deuteronomy | 30:19

Dear Child of Mine,

>I want you to choose life. Choosing life means looking at life
with hope and love rather than with fear and doubt.

Choosing life means caring about others instead of obsessing
about yourself. Choosing life means watching a sunset or
encouraging a friend, instead of vegging out in front of the TV set
every night. Choosing life means trusting Me to help you do the
hard things, instead of giving up before you even try. Choosing
life is laughing with children instead of doubting with skeptics.
Choosing life is celebrating your own gifts instead of being
envious of someone else's.

Choosing life means standing for what's right and true, even if
someone thinks you're a geek for doing it. Choosing life is loving
Me.

Yours for Life,
>God

=== ===============

LET ME BE YOUR TREE HOUSE

**You are my hiding place; you will protect
me from trouble and surround
me with songs of deliverance.**

| | | Psalm ▼ | 32:7 ▼ | | | |

————————————

My Child,

>Is there a special place you go to get away from everything and everybody? Some people like to climb a tree. Others hide away in a corner of their backyard. Concealing yourself in a physical place helps when people and circumstances are just too much for you.

But where can you hide from your emotions and fears? Let Me be your hiding place. When things get rough, run to Me when you need shelter from your life. Pray and read My words in the Bible. Then listen. Not only will I shelter you, I will surround you with encouraging songs. I will sing you back to peace. Come away with Me to our secret place. I'll meet you there.

Your Shelter,
>God

=== ===============

WHAT TO WEAR EVERY DAY

Clothe yourselves with compassion, kindness, humility, gentleness, and patience.

| Colossians ▼ | 3:12 ▼ |

— — — — — — — — — — — — —

Dear Child,

>You might think that I have a certain dress code for you when you come to church ... like maybe I demand your best outfit and your hair combed just right. Actually, I'm not all that concerned about things like that. Styles change every year.

Here's the wardrobe I want you to wear every day, and not just on Sundays: I want you to wear compassion—a kind heart that sympathizes with others. I want you to wear kindness—simple deeds that help make other people's lives easier. I want you to wear humility—an attitude that isn't pushy. I want you to wear gentleness and patience—a gracious tolerance that doesn't demand its own way.

Those things will never go out of style, and you'll always be well dressed.

Your Heavenly Father,
>God

=== ================

I AM WITH YOU

**The Lord is close to the brokenhearted and
saves those who are crushed in spirit.**

Psalm ▼ 34:18 ▼

Dear Child,

>My Son Jesus hung out with brokenhearted people—two sisters
who had just lost their brother, a man whose young son had died,
another man who'd been blind his whole life, a little shrimp of a
tax collector who was hated by everybody ... the list goes on and
on. He was close to the people who needed Him, and so am I.

Sadness is not new to Me. I have experienced the death of My
Son. I know what it's like to be sad. So if you're sad, you are not
alone. If you feel like you just can't go on, turn to Me. I am here to
dry your tears and ease your pain. I care for you.

Your Lord,
>God

=== ================

GET CAUGHT DOING IT RIGHT

**Whatever you do, work at it with all your heart,
as working for the Lord, not for men ....
It is the Lord Christ you are serving.**

Colossians ▼ 3:23–24 ▼

My Child,

>When no one is looking, it's tempting to cheat. Maybe you wouldn't even call it cheating. Maybe you'd just call it slacking, or easing off.

But to make a habit of slacking is to lose the joy in your work. Doing a job right makes you feel good, because I made you to enjoy hard work—to enjoy doing your best.

So don't work hard because you think I'm standing over you cracking the whip. I'm not. Don't even work hard to please other people. Do your best whether people are watching you or not. Then when your boss or teacher does pop in unexpectedly, they'll wonder why you're working so hard. But we'll know why. It'll be our secret!

Your Heavenly Employer,
>God

=== ==============

MY OFFER STILL STANDS

Yes, and from ancient days I am he. No one can deliver out of my hand. When I act, who can reverse it?

Isaiah | 43:13

_____

Dear Child,

>Don't you hate it when people promise something good, and then they change their minds? "Oh, I would have bought that for you, but they raised the price." "I know I said I'd be there, but something important came up." I'm not like that. If I say I'll be there, I'll be there.

When I do something, no one can undo it. I have chosen you to be part of My family, and that offer is always open. I will never withdraw it. I want to spend as much time with you as I can. I am never too busy for you—ever! I love you, and I always want to be with you. That will never change.

Your Promise-Keeper,
>God

=== ===============

I'LL MEET YOU IN YOUR ROOM

**In my Father's house are many rooms; if it
were not so, I would have told you.
I am going there to prepare a place for you.
And if I go and prepare a place for you,
I will come back and take you to be with me
that you also may be where I am.**

John ▼   14:2–3 ▼

— — — — — — — — — — — —

Dear Child of Mine,

>My Son, Jesus, can't lie. So when He says there's a home in
Heaven for those who follow Him, it's true.

Heaven is real—as real as anything you can touch right now. It's
actually more real, because it will last forever, and the stuff you
can touch now will eventually turn to dust.

So what's up here? Well, I have a room all ready for you. All the
things you love are in it, and some things are there that you will
love and don't even know about yet. Ever heard of sky-blading?
Never mind. You'll see.

The best news is, I'm here waiting for you. When you're finally
home with Me, it will be awesome forever. I'm looking forward to
seeing you face to face, but first, you've got a lot of living to do
on earth. So hang in there!

Your Heavenly Father,
>God

=== ================

GET REAL

Are you tired? Worn out? Burned out on religion? Come to me. Get away with me and you'll recover your life. I'll show you how to take a real rest.

Matthew ▼ 11:28 MSG ▼

_ _ _ _ _ _ _ _ _ _ _ _ _ _ _

My Child,

>There is nothing more exhausting than "playing church," acting like you've got it all together while inside you're aching, lonely, and needing to be real with someone. That kind of religious "play acting" is the road to spiritual burnout.

Besides, it's not how things work with Me. Never has been. If there's one place on earth you can be real, it's with Me. If there's one place you can give the act a rest, it's in My presence. I'm not interested in anyone's performance. I want to make contact with the real you. I want to heal what's hurting in you, to forgive what needs forgiving, to refresh you totally. Come away with Me and let Me fill you with new life. Give it a rest.

Your Heavenly Dad,
>God

=== ================

I ANSWER PRAYER

Jesus answered ... "Whatever you ask for in prayer, believe that you have received it, and it will be yours."

| Mark | 11:22, 24 |

- - - - - - - - - - - - - -

Dear Child,

>Will I give you everything you ask for? Well, answering prayers is My business. Some people say, "Be careful what you pray for, because it just might happen." I say, "if you pray according to what I want, it will happen."

Now don't come to Me with a prayer about wanting the universe to fit into your baseball glove or wanting to own all the cars in America. Get real. But if there's something you want to ask Me— something you just can't get out of your head—then that prayer is probably from Me. Pray it back to Me and believe that I'll answer it.

Remember, I can do anything. No one has ever trusted Me too much. Just ask Me.

The Giver,
>God

=== ================

SAY THE WELCOMING WORD

It's the word of faith that welcomes God to go to work
and set things right for us .... Say the welcoming
word to God—"Jesus is my Master"—
embracing, body and soul. . .. You're not "doing"
anything; you're simply calling out to God, trusting
him to do it for you. That's salvation.

Romans ▼   10:9-10 MSG ▼

- - - - - - - - - - - - - - -

My Child,

>Some people have a totally wrong idea of what it is to have
a relationship with Me. They come at Me with all sorts of
accomplishments, trying to impress Me with what good people
they are. (If they're so good, what do they need Me for?)

Don't they realize I'm already aware of their mistakes?
Approaching Me with a false pride is not the way to impress Me.
I want to be friends with the person who'll go out on a limb and
express faith in Me and My Son ... the person who'll welcome our
work ... the person who's not too proud to show need.

You don't need to wear a religious mask or put on a big charade.
When you tell Jesus you believe in Him and need Him, you can
walk right in My front door. It's that simple.

Lord of All,
>God

=== ===============

WHAT WILL HAPPEN WHEN THE STORM COMES

Unless the LORD builds the house, its builders labor in vain.

| Psalm | 127:1 |

- - - - - - - - - - - - - - -

Dear Child,

>In some parts of the world, where storms are terrible and regular, people build their houses out of bamboo and paper. Every year or so, storms wipe out everything. Because the people realize their houses are just going to get knocked down, they don't waste their time and effort trying to build strong houses. This is smart.

You can't build a strong, successful life all on your own. Apart from Me, you'll work to make your life look good, but something will always come along to knock it down. I am the only One with enough power and wisdom to build a life that will withstand the storms.

So get smart. Forget your own plans. Let Me show you My plans and help you build a strong, successful life. My work lasts.

The Master Architect,
>God

=== ===============

CAN I HELP?

**Commit to the Lord whatever you do,
and your plans will succeed.**

Proverbs ▼ 16:3 ▼

Dear Child,

>I want to be involved in your life—not just your prayer life or your church life—but your whole life. Even if you're just training your dog, or writing a story, or decorating your room, every activity goes better with Me.

If what you're doing is not wrong, then bring it to Me and ask for My help. Think about it: I painted every sunset and created all the flowers, so I'm pretty handy at helping to decorate a room. When you commit a project to Me, I'll work with you to make it better. I'm not as interested in the project as I am in our relationship. I love doing things with you. I want to be a part of your whole life. Please share your plans with Me.

Your Creator,
>God

I STILL SHOW UP IN PERSON

Jesus answered: ... "Anyone who has seen me has seen the Father."

John ▼ 14:9 ▼

- - - - - - - - - - - - - -

My Dear Child,

>Why don't I show up in person and let everybody see how real I am? I did! Instead of just looking down from Heaven, I came to earth myself in the life of My Son, Jesus.

Jesus was born to simple parents and lived in a small village. He went to school and learned a trade. Then he spent three years telling people about Me. For that, He was arrested, tried, found guilty, beaten, spit on, and nailed to a cross where He suffered and died. Some friends buried Him in a borrowed tomb, but by the power of My Holy Spirit, I brought Him back to life to live forever!

In Jesus, I showed up in person. And I'm still showing up in the lives of those who trust Me and let Me work in their lives.

Personally,
>God

=== ===============

MAKE A ROAD IN YOUR HEART

Prepare a road for the Lord to travel on! Widen the pathway before him! Level the mountains! Fill up the valleys! Straighten the curves! Smooth out the ruts! And then mankind shall see the Savior sent from God.

Luke | 3:4–6 TLB

My Child,

>I want you to make a road in your heart which Jesus can travel on. With the help of My Holy Spirit, cut down all the undergrowth of meaningless activities. Level the mountains of self-centeredness and conceit. Fill up the valleys of low self-worth and depression. Straighten out any crooked motives or twisted justifications. Smooth out the ruts of procrastination and laziness.

With a smooth road to travel on, Jesus can move freely through your life, making the kind of difference He longs to make in you. He can lead and guide you, and you will find a new freedom to follow Him. And the more you follow Him, the more you will be like Him. Then the people around you will be able to see Him in you!

Your Way-Maker,
>God

=== ================

THE LAMB THAT WAS A LION

He was led like a lamb to the slaughter, and as a sheep before her shearers is silent, so he did not open his mouth.

Isaiah 53:7

- - - - - - - - - - - - - - -

Dear Child,

>Jesus lived a perfect life as a human being. Before He left Heaven, I gave Him a job to do on earth, and He did it exactly like I told Him.

After He was tortured and handed over to be crucified, Jesus had a chance to defend Himself. After all, He was perfectly innocent. And He was so powerful, He could have destroyed all of His accusers by just waving His hand ... but He didn't. Jesus obeyed Me and kept His mouth shut so that He would die on the cross, taking all your mistakes and wrongdoing with Him. His sacrificial death earned you the chance to know My forgiveness ... and Me.

So understand, the strongest person isn't the one who blows up everything or yells the loudest about how unfair life is. The strongest person is the one who silently obeys Me, even in the face of false accusations. Be strong by being humble.

The Father of Jesus,
>God

=== ===============

GET SET FREE

Then you will know the truth, and the truth will set you free.

| | | | John | ▼ | 8:32 | ▼ | | |

My Child,

>Truth is the most freeing thing in the world. When you know the truth and live your life by it, you don't have to make up any excuses or alibis.

When you live in a truthful way, you aren't saying something to one person and something else to another person and then trying to remember what you said to whom. You can speak your mind and show your feelings without fear. You can simply be yourself and know it's enough.

I want you to know the truth deep inside yourself, so that you don't have to waste your energy untangling a lot of lies, fibs, and half-truths. I want you to experience the freedom that comes with being totally honest. Most of all, I want you to know Jesus. He is the Truth.

Your Father,
>God

=== ===============

IT'S THE TRUTH

**Every word of God is flawless; he is a shield
to those who take refuge in him.
Do not add to his words, or he will
rebuke you and prove you a liar.**

Proverbs | 30:5–6

Dear Child,

>If I said it in My Book, the Bible, then you can believe it's true. I can't lie. You can put all your faith in Me. The problem is, people just don't believe Me enough.

Will you trust Me? Then pray to Me. Trust Me by doing things My way, even when it doesn't seem to make sense. Some doubters say My Book is full of fairy tales. They try to explain away My miracles as if they didn't happen. But they did happen.

Put Me to the test yourself. I protect people who rely on Me. The best way to find out if I'm really "the net under your trapeze" is to let go and go for it. If you fall, I'll catch you. Really! Every promise in the Bible is true. Try Me and see.

Your Trustworthy Friend,
>God

=== ===============

IT'S OKAY TO HAVE DOUBTS

Then he said to Thomas, "Put your finger here;
see my hands. Reach out your hand and put it
into my side. Stop doubting and believe."
Thomas said to Him, "My Lord and my God!"

| John | ▼ | 20:27–28 | ▼ |

My Child,

>Jesus is not surprised by your doubts. Even His disciples
doubted Him sometimes. After His crucifixion, Jesus shocked
them all by showing up in person. To prove Who He was, He let
them touch the wounds in His hands where the nails had been
driven, and the wound in His side where He had been stabbed.
They were convinced.

They couldn't wait to tell Thomas, who hadn't been with them
when Jesus appeared. But Thomas said, "Sorry, I'm not taking
your word for it. I've got to see this for myself." One week later,
Jesus showed up again, and the first thing He said was, "Come
on over here, Thomas. See for yourself. Touch My wounds."
That's all it took. Thomas believed.

So don't feel bad when you have doubts. Jesus wants to help
you believe in Him. So do I.

Your Father,
>God

=== ===============

TRUST ME IN THE HARD TIMES

Though he slay me, yet will I hope in him.

| | Job ▼ | 13:15 ▼ | |

_____

My Child,

>Job was a man who lived more than three thousand years ago. He had a pretty horrible life for a while. All of his children died on the same day. Then he got a horrible skin disease that was so bad, he scratched his sores with broken pottery just to get some relief. And he lost everything he owned.

All Job's friends told him to just curse Me and die. But Job said, "Even if God kills me, I will still trust Him." Job knew that I was good. He also knew that he had done nothing wrong. Job didn't know why he was suffering, and he questioned Me. But Job never gave up on Me.

If you have unanswered questions, that's all right. Someday you will understand everything. But for now please believe that I love you, and don't give up on Me. Trust Me in the hard times.

Your Faithful Friend,
>God

=== ===============

WATCH HOW I DO IT

Walk with me and work with me—watch how I do it. Learn the unforced rhythms of grace. I won't lay anything heavy or ill-fitting on you. Keep company with me and you'll learn to live freely and lightly.

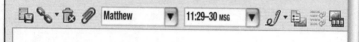

Matthew   11:29-30 MSG

— — — — — — — — — — — — — — —

My Child,

>Some people will do everything they can to complicate the life of faith. They'll try to strangle you with rules and trip you up with regulations. And they'll appoint themselves as watch dogs of your faith if you let them.

Steer clear of those people! If you don't, they'll strip the beauty and freedom out of your heart as quickly as I pour it in. The best way to learn to travel the faith journey is to walk with Me. The surest way to figure out how it works is to work with Me.

There is a freedom that you'll learn to put on every day—a freedom tailor-made for you. There's a dance of grace so joyful it makes you feel like you're flying. Watch and follow Me.

Love always,
>God

=== ================

LIVE YOUR LIFE

We can say without any doubt or fear, "The Lord is my Helper and I am not afraid of anything that mere man can do to me."

	Hebrews	▼	13:6 TLB	▼	

_ _ _ _ _ _ _ _ _ _ _ _ _ _ _

My Child,

>Don't lock your heart away in a safe little room because you're afraid of being hurt. It will become a jail cell for you. And a heart that's locked in jail will never learn to live.

I want you to unlock your emotions. Take on a challenge. Move out into the flow of life and invest your feelings in other people. Sure, it may be risky. I'm not saying that everything you try will be painless or work out perfectly. You will get hurt from time to time. Your heart may get broken.

But whatever happens, I will be with you to heal your hurts and put your broken heart back together. Don't bury your life ... live it!

The Lord of Life,
>God

=== ===============

I GIVE THE HOLY SPIRIT

And if the Spirit of him who raised Jesus from the dead is living in you, he who raised Christ from the dead will also give life to your mortal bodies through his Spirit, who lives in you.

Romans ▾ 8:11 ▾

My Child,

>What if the spirit of Michael Jordan possessed you and suddenly you could play basketball just like him? You probably wouldn't be as tall as he is, but I imagine your game would improve considerably. Your friends would say, "Man, where did you learn to do that!"

Becoming a Christian means that you are possessed by My Spirit—the Holy Spirit. It may sound scary, but it's really a great thing. My Spirit comes to live inside of you. My Spirit possessed Jesus and raised Him from the dead. So if My Holy Spirit is that powerful and that good, don't you want Him living in you? My Spirit in you will do things through you that you could never do alone.

Ask My Spirit into your life. I want to empower you.

Your One and Only Lord,
>God

=== ===============

DEPEND ON ME

Jesus Christ is the same yesterday and today and forever.

Hebrews ▼ 13:8 ▼

– – – – – – – – – – – – – –

My Child,

>A lot of kids you know probably run their lives based on their feelings. Maybe they've been taught to believe that being true to their feelings means they are being true to themselves. But think about it. Feelings are the most unpredictable, undependable things in the world.

If the gauges in your car registered your feelings, one minute your engine would be running hot, and the next minute, cold. One minute the gauge would show a full tank of gas, and the next minute you would be on empty.

But My character, My strength, and My love are unchangeable. I love you today and that is never going to change. It's so much better to run your life based on the steady, unchangeable gauges of Who I am and how much I love you. Depend on Me.

Your Father,
>God

=== ================

I'M TALKING TO YOU

**Listen and hear my voice;
pay attention and hear what I say.**

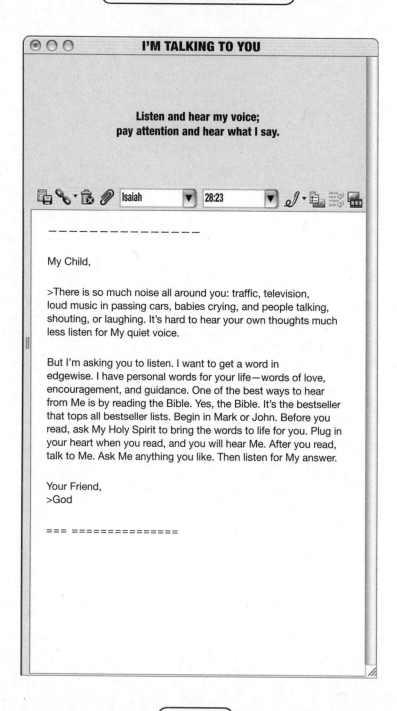

Isaiah ▼ 28:23 ▼

— — — — — — — — — — — — — — —

My Child,

>There is so much noise all around you: traffic, television,
loud music in passing cars, babies crying, and people talking,
shouting, or laughing. It's hard to hear your own thoughts much
less listen for My quiet voice.

But I'm asking you to listen. I want to get a word in
edgewise. I have personal words for your life—words of love,
encouragement, and guidance. One of the best ways to hear
from Me is by reading the Bible. Yes, the Bible. It's the bestseller
that tops all bestseller lists. Begin in Mark or John. Before you
read, ask My Holy Spirit to bring the words to life for you. Plug in
your heart when you read, and you will hear Me. After you read,
talk to Me. Ask Me anything you like. Then listen for My answer.

Your Friend,
>God

=== ================

THINGS LOOK GREAT FROM UP HERE

It is God who arms me with strength and makes
my way perfect. He makes my feet like the feet of
a deer; he enables me to stand on the heights.

Psalm | 18:32–33

——————————————

Dear Child,

>If you could be either a submarine captain or an airplane pilot, which would you be? Most people say they would want to be a pilot, but why? Well, the view certainly is better. In a plane, you get a sense of perspective. You are above the action, not under it.

Do you ever feel like you're drowning in the events of your own life? When you get that underwater feeling, I want to lift you up and give you My birds-eye view of your life. I can see into the future, and I know how everything's going to work out.

Talk to Me. Ask Me questions, and then find My answers in the Bible. Once you begin to see that I'm in control, you'll feel lifted up. Let Me change your point of view.

Your Strength-Giver,
>God

=== ================

THERE'S ALWAYS A WAY OUT

God is faithful; he will not let you be tempted beyond what you can bear. But when you are tempted, he will also provide a way out so that you can stand up under it.

| 1 Corinthians | 10:13 |

My Child,

>Have you ever complained, "That's not fair," or "That's impossible?" "How does God expect me to be good in this situation? Anyone would give in."

I will never put you in a situation where you're forced to do wrong. I didn't say you wouldn't be tempted to do wrong. When a teacher leaves the room during a test, who's not tempted to cheat? But it's not necessary. When you find yourself in a situation in which you're seriously considering doing the wrong thing, look for My way out. Pray and say, "God, get me out of here!" I will deliver you from the temptation every time. When I show you the way out, take it and run. I am faithful.

Your Deliverer,
>God

=== ==============

I GIVE NEW HOPE

**[The Lord] has sent me
to bind up the brokenhearted.**

Isaiah ▼ 61:1 ▼

Dear Child,

>Have you ever seen a dog after his master dies? Sometimes the dog will mope around the house and howl for days. His entire purpose in life is gone. That dog is brokenhearted.

A brokenhearted person has hoped and been betrayed. Can anyone mend a heart that's been broken? My Son can do it. He knows all about your hopes and dreams. He knows how you've been hurt, and He knows how to give you hope again. If you will trust Jesus to heal your hurt, He will come in and give you a new heart. All you have to do is ask.

Your Heart-Mender,
>God

=== ================

LET YOUR ACTIONS DO THE TALKING

Dear children, let us not love with words or tongue but with actions and in truth.

| 1 John | 3:18 |

Dear Child,

>Here's a little "pop quiz." Suppose a girl was dying of thirst by the side of the road and two of her friends came along.

The first one looked down at the thirsty girl and said, "Oh, I hate to see you suffering like this. I'd love to help you out, but I'm late for a hair appointment. Sorry." But the second girl ran home, got a thermos of cold water, and ran back. She held the water to the thirsty girl's lips and helped her drink. Now the question. Which of the two girls was a true friend? The one who talked a good game, or the one who brought the water?

So what's My point? Keep words to a minimum and let your actions do the talking.

Your Father and Friend,
>God

=== ===============

HAVE A LITTLE FAITH

We live by faith, not by sight.

2 Corinthians | 5:7

My Child,

>You may think you're a person who lacks faith, but you have more faith than you think you do. You use it every day in a million little ways.

For instance, do you test the strength of a chair to see if it will hold you before sitting down? No, you have faith that it will hold your weight. Do you run a lab test on your food before eating it to make sure it isn't poisoned? No, you have faith that the food is safe, so you chow down.

If you needed visual, scientific proof of everything before you acted on it, you'd turn into a paranoid freak who couldn't make a decision. But you don't. You live by faith in lots of other things. How about putting a little faith in Me where it can do some good!

The Invisible,
>God

=== ===============

DON'T COUNT SHEEP, PRAY!

On my bed I remember you; I think of you through the watches of the night.

| Psalm | 63:6 |

--- --- --- --- --- --- --- --- ---

My Dear Child,

>If you can't sleep at night, pray. If the devil is keeping you awake, just pray. He'll get off your case; I guarantee it.

Sometimes I'll wake you up at night. Don't wonder about it—just pray your way back to sleep. Sometimes someone on the other side of the world needs prayer, and I will wake you up to pray for them. If you wake up late at night, ask Me, "Lord, what is it?" I will tell you how to pray, and then you pray that way. It doesn't have to make sense why or who.

Remember, I never sleep. So don't be surprised if you wake up in the night and find Me there. Make Me part of your nighttime, too.

Your Lord,
>God

=== ================

I WILL LIFT YOU UP

Humble yourselves before the Lord, and he will lift you up.

James	▼	4:10	▼

My Child,

>Look around you. Who are the people that are the most stressed out and unhappy? Aren't they the ones who are constantly trying to beat other people out? The ones who put other people down to make themselves look good?

Let Me tell you a secret. You can be a winner without putting anybody down. You can pull for others instead of trying to beat them out. Your only competition should be between yourself as you are and yourself as you want to be. In that competition, your own progress will be your prize.

As you learn to always pull for others without pushing yourself to the front, you'll find that I'll lift you up.

Your Father,
>God

=== ===============

BEING A CHRISTIAN IS SIMPLE, NOT EASY

These are written that you may believe that Jesus is the Christ, the Son of God, and that by believing you may have life in his name.

| John | 20:31 |

My Child,

>Becoming a Christian is not hard. In fact it is so simple any child can do it. If you believe that Jesus is My Son Who came to forgive people and you want to be forgiven, then you can be a Christian.

Although becoming a Christian is simple, living like one can be difficult at times. Standing up for what's right when everyone else is doing what's wrong is hard. Caring about people who don't treat you with any respect is hard. Being My person in places where people don't believe in Me or honor My words is hard.

But the good news is that when you make the simple decision to follow My Son, I am there to help you through the hard times.

Your Redeemer,
>God

=== ===============

TRUST ME

Let us hold unswervingly to the hope we profess, for he who promised is faithful.

Hebrews	10:23

My Child,

>There's a saying, "Who can you trust these days?" Maybe you don't trust your parents, your friends, or even the leaders at your church. Maybe you have a good reason to distrust them.

However, the question is, do you trust Me? If anyone ever hurt you, that was not me. I will never hurt you. In fact I hate it when you're hurt. Know that I exist, that I'm powerful enough to save you, and that I love you intensely. People may let you down, but I never will.

Don't stop trusting Me just because some Christians do cruel or stupid things. I am faithful. My words in the Bible are true. Don't give up on Me, because I will never give up on you.

Your Faithful Father,
>God

=== ================

WANT MY OPINION?

He has showed you, O man, what is good.
And what does the Lord require of you?
To act justly and to love mercy and to
walk humbly with your God.

Micah   ▼   6:8   ▼

—————————————————

Dear Child,

>What's important to you? Some people think money is the name of the game. They keep up with the latest investment schemes so they can score big bucks. Some people think outward appearances are where it's at. They invest everything in trying to look good.

Are you interested in My opinion? Three things really matter to Me: First, I want you to act justly. When you make a promise, keep it. Stand by your beliefs. Second, I want you to love mercy. That means you can't hold grudges. You have to be willing to forgive. And third, I want you to live humbly with Me, not always wanting your own way, but learning to want mine. It means knowing you are My child.

Your Father,
>God

=== ===============

I KNOW YOU BETTER THAN YOU KNOW YOURSELF

**All a man's ways seem right to him,
but the Lord weighs the heart.**

Proverbs ▾ 21:2 ▾

————————————

Dear Child,

>Do you realize that you can think you're right and still be totally wrong? Have you ever argued, "The movie starts at seven-fifteen, I'm sure of it!" And then you show up, and the movie has been on since six o'clock? Or maybe you've convinced yourself that you're being nice to someone for the right reasons, but really you're just being nice to them to copy their homework.

Whatever it is, you may fool yourself and others, but you can't fool Me. I can see right through to the core of your heart. I know when you're being honest, and when you're just lying to yourself. If you really want to know right from wrong, don't trust yourself. Trust Me. Trust My Bible. I'll never lie to you.

Your Conscience,
>God

=== ===============

DON'T WASTE TIME

**Teach us to number our days aright, that
we may gain a heart of wisdom.**

| Psalm | 90:12 |

Dear Child,

>"Time is of the essence." I'm sure you've heard that expression before. It just means that time matters.

Do you realize that this is the only today you'll ever have? You can't live in yesterday, and you can't live in tomorrow. You can only live now. With that in mind, don't waste your time. You only have so much of it. It may seem like you will live forever on earth, but you won't. So why waste time on destructive feelings like anger and bitterness? Learn to forgive.

Don't waste time doing unimportant things. Sure, have fun ... relax. But don't just sit around. I have wonderful things for you to accomplish and experience, and you won't discover them by sitting in front of the television all day. I have something better for you.

The Creator of Time,
>God

=== ===============

JESUS DIDN'T LIVE IN A PALACE

I will put my dwelling place among you, and I will not abhor you. I will walk among you and be your God, and you will be my people.

Leviticus 26:11-12

My Child,

>One time in France, the workers were rioting because they had no more bread to eat. The clueless queen heard about it and said, "Well, just let them eat cake." She was so used to being surrounded by wealth and luxury that she couldn't even imagine people with no food at all.

Some people think I'm like that queen. "God lives in Heaven. How can He know what we humans are going through?" But I do know, because I chose to live with you. So much so, that My Son, Who is God, too, became a man. He didn't just visit earth, He became a human. On the cross, Jesus felt all the hurt any man can ever feel. So yes, I feel your pain. I know what it's like.

I am with you.

Your Father,
>God

=== ================

YOU ARE FREE!

**Christ has set us free to live a free life.
So take your stand! Never again let anyone
put a harness of slavery on you.**

Galatians ▼	5:1 MSG ▼

— — — — — — — — — — — — — —

My Child,

>Jesus paid with His blood to give you spiritual freedom. He blazed a trail from chains to liberty. He paid the ultimate price to cut you loose from the "shoulds" and "oughts" of the religious police.

Here's how to live free: Know that I am real. You don't have to hope I'm real or pretend I'm real. I am real!

Get to know Me. How? Prayer is a great way. So is Bible reading. But don't make those things into hard-and-fast rules. I won't love you one bit more because you pray or read the Bible a certain amount of time each day. But they will help you to know Me better. That will be the payoff.

Love everyone—even those who don't understand the free life. And finally, don't let anyone put you into a spiritual straight jacket. You are free!

Your Emancipator,
>God

=== ================

JUST COME TO ME

I do not concern myself with great matters or things too wonderful for me. But I have stilled and quieted my soul; like a weaned child with its mother.

Psalm ▼ 131:1–2 ▼

Dear Child of Mine,

>Some people are curious. They want to understand how everything works, and that's good. But no one will ever fully understand Me. You'll go crazy trying to prove to someone that I really exist!

You don't need to know everything about Me in order to trust Me though. Think about a light switch. I bet you don't fully understand how a light switch triggers electrons to run down a wire and power a lightbulb. Even electricians and physicists are amazed at how this works. But that doesn't keep you from turning on the lights.

Trust Me. I work for you. I am real. So come to Me as a little child and let Me meet your needs. You don't need to prove My existence to be My friend.

Just Know that I Am,
>God

=== ===============

LEARN TO BE A LOVE RECEIVER

I tried keeping rules and working my head off to please God, and it didn't work. So I quit being a "law man" so that I could be God's man.

| Galatians ▾ | 2:19 MSG ▾ |

Dear Child,

>Unless you can obey every law down to the last letter, you can't say that you've kept the law. And no one can keep every letter of every law. So no one can make it as a law keeper. You can't get in good with Me by working hard enough either.

So if you can't earn your way into My heart by being good enough or working hard enough, what can you do? You can only be mine by accepting and embracing My love. I've made it so simple that it actually makes some people mad. They'd rather do something for Me than receive what I've done for them. They'd rather give Me something than receive the gift I have for them.

The truth remains—you can only be God's man or woman when you learn to be a love receiver.

Your Father,
>God

=== ================

I BRING THE JOY

The Sovereign Lord ... has sent me to ... provide for those who grieve in Zion—to bestow on them a crown of beauty instead of ashes, the oil of gladness instead of mourning, and a garment of praise instead of a spirit of despair.

Isaiah 61:1-3

— — — — — — — — — — — —

My Child,

>You know you're sad when you're at Disney World in the middle of all the color and excitement, and you still feel empty inside. Maybe you feel that way sometimes. But when it seems that nothing will cheer you up, turn to Jesus!

Jesus might not bring you a gift or make a funny face, but He'll make you glad on the inside where it really counts. He can change your perspective, because where He is, there is joy. Ask Jesus to come and cheer up your heart. Give Him your depression—your ashes—and let Him crown you with beauty.

I am glad, and I want you to be glad ... not a fake-smile kind of glad, but a deep-down-in-your-heart kind of glad.

Your Joy-Giver,
>God

=== ==============

A PROVEN FRIEND

My command is this: Love each other as I have loved you. Greater love has no one than this, that he lay down his life for his friends.

John | 15:12-13

_____

Dear Child,

>Do you have a best friend? Would you be willing to die for her or him? It's easy to say yes now, but what if someone had a gun to your head? Is there anyone in your life that you love so much you would die for them?

Jesus loves you that much, and to prove it, He actually did die for you. He died so that you would know He was your friend. Jesus is not just some spooky, holy, faraway guy with white robes and a beard. He's Someone Who wants to call you friend. You can talk to Him when you pray and tell Him about your day. You can tell Him what you like and what you don't like.

Get to know Jesus as your friend. Hang out with My Son. He's great company!

Jesus' Dad,
>God

=== ===============

RESPECT HIS HOLY HOUSE

You realize, don't you, that you are the temple of God, and God himself is present in you? No one will get by with vandalizing God's temple, you can be sure of that.

1 Corinthians ▼ 3:16–17 MSG ▼

― ― ― ― ― ― ― ― ― ― ― ― ― ― ―

Dear Child of Mine,

>Your body is the holy place where My Son wants to live. He only needs to be invited in, and He will make His home in you.

Once Jesus has moved in, He will want you to treat His house (your body) as a place of honor. Just like you wouldn't want someone walking into your house and throwing a lot of trash around or writing on the walls, He won't want you or anyone else treating your body with disrespect because He will be living there. What you eat, drink, read, watch, and think about—all of those go into My Son's home.

Make sure that you only invite in what will please Him. And make sure your friends understand the house rules, too! Welcome Jesus home today!

Your Creator,
>God

=== ===============

I AM HERE FOR YOU

**He was despised and rejected by men,
a man of sorrows, and familiar with suffering.
Like one from whom men hide their faces he
was despised, and we esteemed him not.**

Isaiah 53:3

‒ ‒ ‒ ‒ ‒ ‒ ‒ ‒ ‒ ‒ ‒ ‒ ‒ ‒

Child of Mine,

>Maybe you think Jesus never got His feelings hurt. Maybe you think He didn't even have feelings like you do because He was God.

Well, He was God, but He was also a human being. So He felt hurt and rejected when people were cruel to Him. I'll tell you something else: When people hurt Him, they were hurting Me, too. It's the same with you. When people hurt you, they hurt Me. When your heart is breaking, My heart is breaking.

So on one of those really crummy days when you feel like your heart's been kicked around like a football and nobody cares—remember, I care. Come to Me, and I'll comfort you just like I comforted Jesus. I am here for you.

Your Comforter,
>God

=== ================

LET LOVE TAKE OVER

There is no room in love for fear. Well-formed love banishes fear. Since fear is crippling, a fearful life—fear of death, fear of judgment— is one not yet fully formed in love.

| 1 John | 4:18 MSG |

My Child,

>Fear is one of the most destructive, paralyzing emotions in the world. It can keep you from fulfilling your dreams—doing the things that will make you the happiest.

Fear hits different people in different ways. Some people fear failure; some fear success. Some fear dying, and others fear living. Some fear the criticism that keeps them from moving forward toward their dreams.

Let Me tell you a secret that will rid your life of fear. A heart that is filled with love has no room for fear. As My love rushes in and takes over, fear has to let go and find another place to hang out. So let Me fill you with My love and watch fear disappear. Love is My specialty!

Love always,
>God

=== ===============

JESUS HAS DESIGNS ON YOUR LIFE

It's in Christ that we find out who we are and what we are living for. Long before we first heard of Christ and got our hopes up, he had his eye on us, had designs on us for glorious living.

Ephesians   1:11 MSG

My Child,

>When you enroll in college, you take an interest and aptitude test to find out what subject you should major in. Those tests can be helpful, but the truth is, you could learn those things (and a whole lot more) just by talking to My Son.

Long before you had even heard of Jesus, He knew all about you. He knew who you would grow up to be. He knew what you'd be most interested in and what you'd be good at. He even had a plan for what part He wanted you to play in life. You can ignore that plan if you want to, but if you do, you'll be missing out on the fun and adventure of discovering your true purpose for living.

Jesus wants to lead you into this adventure. How about it? Are you ready to follow?

Your Guide,
>God

=== ================

THE SECOND ROOM

Jesus said to her, "I am the resurrection and the life. He who believes in me will live, even though he dies."

| | John ▼ | 11:25 ▼ | |

--- --- --- --- --- --- --- --- --- ---

My Child,

>What if you got called out of one of your classes at school to receive a message that someone you love had died—a parent, a grandparent, a sister, a brother, or a good friend? You'd probably rather not think about that.

But eventually you will have to deal with death, because it's a sure thing. But death is not the end for people who believe in Me. It's only a doorway between Earth and Heaven. On earth, there are many beautiful things, as well as trouble and pain. Life in Heaven is filled with eternal beauty, joy, and peace. You don't get to Heaven by being good enough; you only get there by believing in Jesus. He is the door.

Your Eternal Father,
>God

=== ================

THE GIFT THAT CHANGES YOU

**For it is by grace you have been saved, through faith—
and this not from yourselves, it is the gift of God.**

Ephesians	2:8

Dear Child,

>What's holding you back from accepting My free gift of a
new life? Do you think that if you accept, you'll have to change
yourself and be perfect from now on? That I'll be mad if you ever
mess up?

That's not the deal. In fact, it's totally backwards. What I'm
offering you is a gift. A gift is free. You can't earn it with your
good behavior. You don't change to earn the gift. You accept the
gift, and it changes you!

What exactly is the gift? What is this new life all about? It's about
forgiveness, freedom, and friendship with Me. It's about a deeper
happiness than you have ever experienced and an inner feeling
of calm and peace that you can't find anywhere else. Believe in
Me. Receive your free gift!

Your Heavenly Father,
>God

=== ================

BE A JANITOR?

For he who is least among you all—he is the greatest.

Luke   9:48

My Child,

>Titles, accomplishments, and awards don't impress Me. As
a matter of fact, I'm often more impressed by the heart of the
janitor than I am by the president of a company. People at the
top sometimes use others instead of serving others.

But if you're a janitor, whom are you going to use? As a janitor,
you're always serving others. You have to come to work every
day willing to clean up other people's messes. It's that type of
serving that impresses Me. My Son could have come to earth as
a king or a president, but He came as a servant.

When I see someone willing to serve others, I'll put them on top,
because I know I can trust them.

Your Servant,
>God

=== ================

TAKE THAT RISK

Jesus gave them this answer: "I tell you the truth, the Son can do nothing by himself; he can do only what he sees his Father doing, because whatever the Father does the Son also does.

John ▼ 5:19 ▼

— — — — — — — — — — — — —

Dear Child of Mine,

>Lots of people believe that Jesus must have had some kind of big game plan mapped out for His life—that every day He woke up and moved smoothly from point A to point B to point C. Wrong!

Jesus didn't know what He was going to do from one minute to the next! He just kept His eyes on Me, and I gave Him the day's agenda. He woke up each morning, never sure what the day would bring, but willing to listen to Me and do things My way. He knew the Scriptures backwards and forwards.

I want the same kind of life for you, so start by reading My Word. Practice keeping your eyes on Me, and when I show you what to do, take that risk and just do it! Trust Me. My dreams for you are even greater than what you could ever ask or think.

Your Life-Planner,
>God

=== ================

CLONINGER

I'VE GOT A PRESENT FOR YOU

You will fill me with joy in your presence, with eternal pleasures at your right hand.

Psalm ▼ 16:11 ▼

My Child,

>What gives you pleasure? For some, it's a close Superbowl game that goes down to the wire. For others, it's a quiet walk in the park enjoying the spring flowers, or buying the new live CD of their favorite band.

The pleasures of life make you glad to be alive. Now think about eternal pleasures—pleasures that last forever. Many of the world's pleasures get old after just a little while, like a week-old Christmas toy that's no longer any fun. But the pleasures I give never wear out.

Are you interested? Then take some time and get to know Me. The people who know Me are the ones who discover My everlasting pleasures.

Your Gift-Giver,
>God

=== ================

JUST BE YOU

For you created my inmost being; you knit me together in my mother's womb. I praise you because I am fearfully and wonderfully made; your works are wonderful, I know that full well.

Psalm 139:13–14

— — — — — — — — — — — — — —

My Dear Child,

>Sometimes you don't like your looks and you blame Me. You ask, "Why didn't you give me perfect skin like this person or a perfect body like that person?"

You're letting magazines and movies define good looks for you. You're listening to the lies of a money-hungry world. They want to sell you skin treatments and diet books, so they convince you something's wrong with you. Remember when Jesus found money changers doing business in the temple? He went ballistic!

You are the temple in which My Spirit wants to make a home, and it infuriates Me to see these money grubbers trying to sell you a lie. I'm the One Who thought you up, and I love what I made! You're the only you I've got. So just be you!

Your Creator,
>God

=== ================

LET'S TALK TODAY

Before they call I will answer; while they are still speaking I will hear.

Isaiah ▼ 65:24 ▼

— — — — — — — — — — — — — —

Dear Child,

>Prayer is not a process of trying to talk Me into doing something that I don't want to do. Prayer is realizing how willing I am to be involved in your life and how excited I am about involving you in Mine.

The moment you admit in prayer that you've been wrong, I forgive you. In prayer, I can encourage you when you're down and show you the way when you're lost. I can give you courage to face your fears, and I can bend down to dry your tears.

Can't you tell by now how much I want to talk with you? In fact, I'm listening for your prayers day and night. I'm already answering your call while it's still just a thought in your head! Let's talk today.

Your Friend Who Listens,
>God

=== ================

I LOVE YOU FOREVER

"Though the mountains be shaken and the hills be removed, yet my unfailing love for you will not be shaken nor my covenant of peace be removed," says the Lord, who has compassion on you.

Isaiah | 54:10

Dear Child,

>I have chosen you to be Mine. I want to have a relationship with you. Even if you turn from Me—even if you hate Me—I will still love you.

Your attitude and behavior don't change My love for you. If you turn from Me, or cut yourself off from Me, I still want to be with you. It's like when you turn off the faucet. Does the water just disappear out of the pipe? No, it stays there waiting for you to turn on the faucet again. I'm like that water. I'm here waiting. I want you as My child. No disobedience or rebellion on your part can change that.

I have chosen you, and I will never reject you. Please don't cut yourself off from My love.

Your Faithful Father,
>God

WHAT ABOUT EVIL?

**Yet the Lord longs to be gracious to you;
he rises to show you compassion.
For the Lord is a God of justice.
Blessed are all who wait for him!**

Isaiah ▼ 30:18 ▼

My Child,

>Why is there evil in the world? If I'm so powerful, then why do I let bad things happen? It's like this—I've chosen to let people make their own decisions, and many people have decided to go against Me.

Whenever people set themselves against Me and My goodness, that's evil. But I hate evil, and I hate it when people are hurt. The good news is, when people decide to obey Me, to let Me be in control, those people receive My justice.

Has someone done evil to you? I didn't do it. I want to protect you and love you and bless you. Choose Me, and your life will be better, even though you live in a world full of evil. In the end, I will destroy all evil. Until then, choose My way. I love you so much.

The Lord of Justice,
>God

=== ===============

AN ADDED BONUS

**That's my parting gift to you. Peace.
I don't leave you the way you're used to
being left .... So don't be upset.**

John   14:27 MSG

My Child,

>Most people live with chaos and conflict in their lives: outside conflicts with other people and situations, and inside conflicts between different opinions and ideas in their own heads.

Jesus wants to give you peace. When you receive His love, His peace is an added bonus. When you embrace His friendship, you'll be able to set Him, like the sun, in the center of your personal solar system. Then all of the chaotic struggles and conflicts tend to quiet down. All of the questions untangle themselves. All of the things you care about line up and revolve around Jesus, like planets pulled into the orbit of His grace. And He will give you peace.

Peace always,
>God

=== ===============

LET MY WORDS BECOME ACTIONS

If you love me, show it by doing what I've told you.

John   14:15 MSG

— — — — — — — — — — — — —

My Child,

>When you begin to love Me—really love Me—something will happen in your life. You'll fall in love with My words, and My words will show up in your actions.

All the secrets I've shared, the stories I've told, the mysteries I've explained, the guidance I've given will affect you in a daily way. Every aspect of your life will be touched—your decisions, your friendships, your attitudes, and your faith. My words will become like a software program that is downloaded into your heart and mind, and you'll begin to respond to what I've said as easily as a computer responds to the program it's operating.

Life is exciting when My words affect your actions! Let My words make a difference.

Your Programmer,
>God

=== ================

I WILL MEET ALL YOUR NEEDS

**I have learned to be content whatever the circumstances ....
I can do everything through him who gives me strength.**

| | | Philippians ▼ | 4:11,13 ▼ | |

– – – – – – – – – – – – – –

Dear Child,

>Contentment is a valuable commodity. Some people have boats, cars, big houses, and money, but they can't find contentment. What good is all that stuff if they aren't satisfied with it?

Contentment is something that only I can give. Paul, one of My children, spent a lot of his life in jail. But even there, Paul was content because he knew this truth: "Jesus gives me all I need." Despite his circumstances, Paul knew that Jesus would take care of him.

Trust Me to meet your needs, and you will always be content. Only I can meet your needs ... and I will.

The Giver of Contentment,
>God

=== ===============

FRESH INGREDIENTS MAKE THE DIFFERENCE

Summing it all up, friends, I'd say you'll do best by filling your minds ... [with] things true, noble, reputable, authentic, compelling, gracious—the best, not the worst; the beautiful, not the ugly; things to praise, not things to curse.

Philippians ▾ 4:8 MSG ▾

— — — — — — — — — — — — — —

Dear Child,

>Any good cook will tell you that the success of a dish depends on fresh ingredients. Try making a delicious stew out of rancid meat and rotten vegetables, and no matter what spices you add or how long you cook it, you're going to end up with a terrible tasting mess.

Instead, when you begin with good, fresh vegetables and fresh, prime meat and add the right combination of spices, you'll want a second helping! The same principle applies to your life. If you fill your head with rotten ingredients, like violence, hatred, and other trash, you're going to cook up a life that's far from delicious.

Use My favorite recipe: Fill your mind with what is true, beautiful, and good; add My love, then enjoy the best life you've ever tasted!

Your Chef,
>God

=== ==============

SH-H-H-H, SLOW DOWN

This is what the Sovereign Lord, the Holy One of Israel, says: "In repentance and rest is your salvation, in quietness and trust is your strength."

Isaiah | 30:15

Dear Child of Mine,

>Repentance is just a fancy word that means "to turn around." It literally means "to change your mind."

My advice is to change your mind about all the busyness in your life. Most people think the more they plan and the more they do, the safer and stronger they will be. I see it differently. I want you to slow down and take time to be quiet. Rest and trust Me, and I'll help you to be strong and successful anyway. That doesn't mean that you never have to plan or take action, but it does mean that if all you do is plan and try, you're missing out on My best for you.

Taking time out to be with Me during a busy day is always a good idea. As you wait on Me, I'll give you the strength you need. Slow down a little!

Your Advisor,
>God

=== ================

⊙ ○ ○   YOU'LL THANK ME LATER

My son, do not make light of the Lord's discipline, and do not lose heart when he rebukes you, because the Lord disciplines those he loves, and he punishes everyone he accepts as a son.

| Hebrews ▼ | 12:5–6 ▼ |

My Child,

>Think about a marathon runner and his coach. Some days the runner doesn't feel like running, but the coach will motivate the runner to run anyway. The runner might hate his coach during the training period, but on race day, after the victory is won, both runner and coach will rejoice.

I'm your Coach for life. I'll challenge and discipline you in preparation for victory. I have a race for you to run. There are things I want you to accomplish. I value you and your success. I correct you because I love you, and I want you to win. Hang in there and trust Me.

Your Coach,
>God

=== ================

YOU CAN BE LIKE JESUS

For from the beginning God decided that those who came to him ... should become like his Son, so that his Son would be the First, with many brothers.

Romans ▼ 8:29 TLB ▼

——————————————

Dear Child,

>Who do you look like in your earthly family? Your brother, your mother, your sister, your dad? Did you know that when you are adopted as a child into My spiritual family, you resemble your big brother, Jesus?

Not physically, of course, but every day your heart, your thoughts, and your actions remind Me of Him. And the longer you're around Him, the more you act like Him. I want you to care about hurting people with broken hearts and those who are weaker than yourself ... just like He did. Believe Me, I know it's hard. His goodness is impossible to imitate on your own.

But when I fill you with My Holy Spirit, you will have the power to live and love like Jesus. Let Me make you more like Him. I can do it!

Your Loving Father,
>God

=== ================

TRUST ME, NO MATTER WHAT

If we are thrown into the blazing furnace,
the God we serve is able to save us from it .... But
even if he does not, we want you to know,
O king, that we will not serve your gods.

Daniel ▼ 3:17–18 ▼

– – – – – – – – – – – – – –

My Child,

>Once a king tried to force three young men to worship him, but
they wouldn't do it. Why? I told them not to worship anyone but
Me.

Well, the king got angry and decided to burn them to death. So
the three young men told the king, "God is going to save us, but
even if He doesn't, we're still going to obey Him." The end of the
story is, I did save them. But the point of the story is, they were
willing to worship Me whether I saved them or not.

I'm still looking for young people who'll take a stand for Me like
those three did. I'll know that you are truly intense about Me
when you decide to obey Me, not because of what I can do for
you, but simply because you love Me. I love you, too.

Your Deliverer,
>God

=== ===============

NOTHING IS IMPOSSIBLE

For nothing is impossible with God.

Luke ▼ 1:37 ▼

Dear Child of Mine,

>Are you going through something right now that seems totally impossible? The more you worry and stew about it, the more impossible it seems. Have you looked at it from every direction, figured it from every angle, tried everything humanly possible, and still you've struck out? Good!

I've been waiting for you to run out of human answers. Now is the time for faith—faith in Me and My strength. Now is the time to remember that I am with you right in the middle of this problem. And when I am with you, nothing is impossible!

I will bring unlimited possibilities into your "impossible" situations if only you trust Me. I won't let you down. I promise.

Powerfully yours,
>God

=== ================

LOVE JESUS BY LOVING OTHERS

I tell you the truth, whatever you did for one of the least of these brothers of mine, you did for me.

Matthew ▼ 25:40 ▼

My Child,

>Have you ever thought that if you could just see Jesus with your own eyes, it would be easier for you to believe in Him? Would it surprise you to know that you can see Him? In fact you do—every day! You look right into His face, but you don't recognize Him.

He's the janitor at your school and the handicapped boy or girl who always feels left out. He's the teacher no one likes and the kid no one wants to eat lunch with. He's walking on the streets and riding in the traffic. He's the ragged woman with her shopping cart full of junk and the old man selling papers on the corner.

Jesus wears millions of disguises, and He wants you to look for Him in people's faces. If you want to love and serve Jesus ... love and serve another person.

Jesus' Father,
>God

=== ===============

STRENGTH TO GET THE JOB DONE

**He gives strength to the weary and
increases the power of the weak.**

	Isaiah ▼	40:29 ▼	

————————————

Dear Child,

>Have you ever been worn out? Ever felt like you have forty-
eight hours of homework to do, and only four hours in which to
do it? When you're physically and mentally exhausted, call on
Me. I can cut your workload in half!

If you'll stop and listen to Me, I'll show you shortcuts and more
efficient ways to get the job done. Some of the things you're
doing might not even need to be done. Most of all, after spending
time with Me, you'll be strengthened in your mind and body. My
love is like a spiritual vitamin that refreshes and wakes you up.
Five minutes with Me could save you hours of work.

So when you feel like you just can't go on ... don't! Take a break
and let Me renew your strength.

Your Rejuvenator,
>God

=== ================

GIVE WITH ENTHUSIASM

Then a poor widow came by and dropped in two small copper coins .... [Jesus] remarked, "this poor widow has given more than all ... [the rich] combined. For they have given a little of what they didn't need, but she ... has given everything she has."

Luke ▼ 21:2-4 TLB ▼

— — — — — — — — — — — — — — —

My Child,

>Rich people who try to buy My approval by throwing money at Me don't impress Me one bit. If a millionaire only gives Me a hundred dollars, it doesn't excite Me much. That's like pocket change to the rich. But if a really poor person gives Me ten bucks, I love their gift, because I know how much they sacrificed to give.

Let Me share a secret with you. If you want to know what's really important to most people, take a look at how they spend their time and money. The most important thing to Me is not the amount of the gift, but the generous spirit behind the gift and the wholehearted, cheerful way it's given. I want your whole heart.

Enthusiastically,
>God

=== ================

JESUS CAN STILL CALM STORMS

He got up, rebuked the wind and said to the waves, "Quiet! Be still!" Then the wind died down and it was completely calm.

Mark ▼ 4:39 ▼

Dear Child of Mine,

>One night when Jesus and His friends were out at sea, a fierce storm came up and everybody panicked ... everybody except Jesus.

Jesus was zonked out in the back of the boat taking a nap. That didn't go over so well with His friends. They were majorly ticked at Him for sleeping through their big catastrophe. What did Jesus do? He stood up and had a word with the wind and the waves. "Quiet! Chill!" He said, and the storm died down.

Jesus still does awesome things like that. No matter what kind of storm you're caught up in, talk to Jesus about it. Tell Him what you need. He can speak to the circumstances in your life, and you'll know His peace. Let Jesus calm your storms.

Peacefully yours,
>God

=== ===============

AND HE HUFFED, AND HE PUFFED

I have set the Lord always before me. Because he is at my right hand, I will not be shaken.

Psalm ▼ 16:8 ▼

My Child,

>Do you know the story of the "Three Little Pigs"? (I know you're mature, but bear with Me.) The two foolish pigs built their houses out of straw and wood. Those houses were NOT big-bad-wolf-proof. But the wise pig built his house out of bricks, and the wolf couldn't blow that one down.

Now the wise pig wasn't trusting in his masonry skills, and he wasn't trusting in his own strength. He was trusting in one thing—the sturdiness of the brick. If you think that you're clever enough to defeat the devil with your own strength, he will eat you up.

There is only one thing that will keep the devil from defeating you ... putting Me first in your life. Then, like the wise pig, you can laugh at the big bad wolf. So if I were you, I'd trust in Me.

Your Fortress,
>God

=== ===============

GOLD THAT WON'T TARNISH

All good athletes train hard. They do it for a gold medal that tarnishes and fades. You're after one that's gold eternally.

| 1 Corinthians ▼ | 9:25 MSG ▼ |

Dear Child,

>When you train to win a race or a championship for your team, you put in lots of time and practice. You schedule workouts and concentrate on strategy sessions with your coach. You sweat—a lot.

If it all pans out the way you hope, you'll be called to the victor's stand at an awards ceremony. You'll experience the satisfaction of having your hard work payoff. But aside from a feeling of pride, all you'll have to show for it is a tin medal or trophy that's destined to tarnish.

The medal you're training for as you live this life for Me is made of gold that never tarnishes. And the satisfaction you will feel as you enter My Kingdom will come from hearing Me say, "Well done, good and faithful servant!" So go for the gold!

Your Rewarder,
>God

=== ================

I WILL FREE YOU

Let [the prisoners] give thanks to the Lord for his unfailing love and his wonderful deeds for men, for he breaks down gates of bronze and cuts through bars of iron.

Psalm ▼ 107:15–16 ▼

— — — — — — — — — — — —

My Child,

>I hope you never see the inside of a prison, but imagine what it would be like. You'd get a desire to go see a movie. Nope, sorry. You're in prison. Hungry for some pizza? Too bad, all they're serving is soup. This is prison, remember?

When the U.S. prisoners of war were released from North Vietnam and returned to America, many of them got off the plane and kissed the ground. That is how thankful they were to be free. Prison bars aren't the only things that can steal your freedom. Anger, jealousy, worry, and fear will wrap you up in chains.

I want to free you from those negative emotions that keep you locked up. Give those feelings to Me, and then prepare to kiss the ground. I will free you.

Your Liberator,
>God

=== ================

INVITE JESUS IN

**Here I am! I stand at the door and knock.
If anyone hears my voice and opens the door,
I will come in and eat with him, and he with Me.**

Revelation ▾ 3:20 ▾

_ _ _ _ _ _ _ _ _ _ _ _ _ _

My Child,

>Your heart is like a house where you spend every day. It's where you keep all your hopes and dreams, all your feelings and fears.

Some rooms in your heart hold shiny trophies. But other rooms hide the things you're most ashamed of. Because the lock is on the inside, you're the only one who can invite someone into your heart. My Son Jesus is standing outside the door of your heart, knocking. If you invite Him in, I will come in with Him.

Don't worry. We won't be shocked by anything We find. We already know what's in there. We want to help you do some house cleaning, one room at a time. We want to live with you in the house you call your heart, and We will make it a home. Will you open the door? It's up to you.

Your Lord,
>God

=== ===============

LIVE, IN PERSON, JESUS!

But we know that when he appears, we shall be like him, for we shall see him as he is.

1 John | 3:2

Dear Child,

>Don't you wish sometimes that you could just see Me in person? Wouldn't it have been great to be alive when Jesus was on the earth in the flesh? Today people pray and strain their hearts to hear My answer. But back then, you could have asked Jesus a question and heard My answer in an audible voice.

The good news is, Jesus is coming back in person. You will be able to see and hear Him again. He is coming back to earth to take His family, those who love Him, to Heaven. And not only will they be able to see Him, but they will be like Him—pure and full of peace and joy. Are you ready to go?

Your Loving Father,
>God

=== ==============

REFERENCES

ABOUT THE AUTHORS

Claire Cloninger, winner of four Dove Awards for songwriting, also created the phenomenally successful musical *My Utmost for His Highest*. She has authored nine books, including best-sellers *A Place Called Simplicity* and *Dear Abba*.

Curt Cloninger, Claire's son, is employed as the Internet Administrator for Integrity Music and is the worship leader at the Mobile Vineyard Christian Fellowship. He spent two years in Youth With a Mission and has worked as a middle-school teacher, a high-school track coach, and a house parent in a children's home. He and his wife, Julie, are parents of nine-month-old Caroline.

If you have enjoyed this book, or if it has impacted your life, we would like to hear from you.